Just Give Me the Damn Ball!

Just Give Me the Damn Ball!

The Fast Times
and Hard Knocks
of an
NFL Rookie

Keyshawn Johnson
with
Shelley Smith

WARNER BOOKS

A Time Warner Company

Warner Books, Inc., 1271 Avenue of the Americas,
New York, NY 10020

 A Time Warner Company

Printed in the United States of America

Just Give Me the Damn Ball!
was produced by Bishop Books of New York City.

First Printing: May 1997

10 9 8 7 6 5 4 3 2 1

Library of Congress Cataloging-in-Publication Data
Johnson, Keyshawn.
Just give me the damn ball!: the fast times and hard knocks of an NFL rookie /
Keyshawn Johnson with Shelley Smith.
p. cm.
Includes index.
ISBN 0-446-52145-0
1. Johnson, Keyshawn. 2. Football players—United States—Biography.
I. Smith, Shelley, 1958- . II. Title.
GV939.J6132A3   1997
796.332'092—dc21   97-1387
CIP

TO THE LORD SAVIOR JESUS CHRIST,
for when you believe in something and
pray, good things can happen

TO MY MOTHER, VIVIAN JESSIE,
for sticking by me when no one else would,
believing in me from day one

TO MY DAUGHTER, MAIA,
for inspiring me to reach for all I can

TO MYSELF,
for not giving a damn about
what people think

—Keyshawn Johnson

TO DYLANN,
for sharing fifth grade
and soccer season with the Jets

—Shelley Smith

.

Acknowledgments

Thanks to my mother, Vivian Jessie; my auntie, Robbie Townsend, and her daughters, Vickie and Susan; my sisters, Sandra Thomas, Kim Thomas, and Denise Thomas; my brothers, Dennis Thomas and Michael Thomas; my cousin Eric Brown; and all those others who've helped me along the way. Thanks to my coaches, Darryl Holmes, Rob Hager, and Jim Wells, for all the extra meals they snuck to me. Also thanks to coaches Marcus Porter, Tracy Atkins, Paul Knox, Eugene McAdoo, John Robinson, Mike Sanford, and the entire USC staff: James Strom, Mike Riley, Keith Burns, Mike Barry, David Robinson, Doug Smith, Dennis Thurman, Charles White, Rod Marinelli, Joe Barry, Joe Hubbard. Also my thanks to George Raveling. Thanks to the Jets' guys, Richard Mann, Ray Hamilton, Shack Harris, and Dick Haley. And thanks to all the coaches who are now claiming they did coach me. Thanks to my friends, Reynaldo "Skeats" Spalding, Tamecus Peoples, Marlin Lewis, Derrick Hazely, Clifton Hunter (aka "Kippy"), Tousaint Thomas (aka "Tutu"), Lamont Warren, Karim Abdul Jabbar, Chris Miller, Jerome Stanley, Lee Kolligian, Shelley Smith. Thanks to Shikiri Hightower and her family. Thanks to the reporters I like: the late Alan Malamud, Jeff Fellenzer, Tim Layden, Ahmad Rashad, Joe Theismann, Sterling Sharpe, Len Berman, Dan Patrick, Bob Costas, Chris Berman, Stuart Scott, Mike Tirico, Joe McDonnell, Gerald Eskenazi, Mark Cannizzaro, Randy Lange, Bill Rhoden, Steve Serby, Richard Oliver, Jim Hill, and all of you who praised me when I scored touchdowns and criticized me when I celebrated, dropped a pass, and lost a game. You know me, I don't sugarcoat anything—thanks for all the bullshit you wrote all year, which gave me and Shelley such great stuff for this book.—K.J.

A book like this was made possible by many, many people. Thanks mostly to Keyshawn, for trusting me with his dream. Thanks to my editor, Rick Wolff, for guidance and inspiration, and my agent, Michael Carlisle, at the William Morris Agency, and his assistant, Mary Beth Brown. Thanks also to my bosses at ESPN, Howard Katz, John Walsh, Bob Eaton, Vince Doria, Jim Cohen, Steve Anderson and Chuck Salituro, and my bosses over the years at *Sports Illustrated*, Mark Mulvoy, Peter Carry, Jerry Kirshenbaum, Steve Robinson, and Chris Hunt, and to my former colleagues at *Pacific Stars & Stripes* and *The San Francisco Examiner*, especially Charles Cooper. Thanks to the Jets' public relations staff and the Jets' beat writers, Gerald Eskenazi, Mark Cannizzaro, Dave Hutchinson, Randy Lange, Richard Oliver, Paul Needell, Rich Cimini, and Jim Corbett. Thanks to *The New York Times'* columnists George Vecsey, Bill Rhoden, and Dave Anderson for early advice. Thanks also to Rob McMahon, Emi Battaglia, Roy Johnson, Eric Lynch, Matthew Ipsen, Dan Patrick, Chris Berman, Ann Marie Jeffords, David Brovsky, Sterling Sharpe, Tracey Reavis, Anthony Cotton, Jeff Fellenzer, Vanessa Tharp, Mike Tharp, Lee Kolligian, Carrie Chase and the folks at Bishop Books, and Warner's Madeleine Schachter, Esq. Also to the coaches and players from Dorsey High School, especially Reynaldo "Skeats" Spalding, Lamont Warren, Roderick Pleasant,

Marlin Lewis, Derek Hazely, and all the coaches and staff from West Los Angeles College and USC. Thanks to Budge Porter and Lee and Maria Kunz, for starting me on this whole wacky book business. Thanks to my friends—team Hiller, Roemer, Walsh, Whitman Nicholas, Chenault-Leonard, Norton, Pleasant, Spalding, Thomas, and Balderama. A very special thanks to Berj Najarian of the Jets' PR staff, Tamecus Peoples, Kelly Neal, and Jerome Stanley. Also—you dance with me, you dance with my family: Ron and Luanne Smith, Jubal and Zoanne Terry (and baby), the Samulesons in Pender, Nebraska, and Sgt. Vince Elmore.—S.S.

Prologue

Maybe the nightmare is over.

On February 10, 1997, I felt new energy return to my body. Suddenly I felt like playing football again. The Jets announced that they had come to terms with the New England Patriots, and that Bill Parcells was now our guy, not as a consultant or whatever, but as **head coach.** For real. Sealed and finished. No interim, no nothing, no bullshit. Parcells is on board and I can tell you right now, things are going to be different this season. Very different.

For one, Parcells commands respect. He's got mine. Hell, he didn't even *like* Patriots wide receiver Terry Glenn, and Terry caught 90 passes and helped lead them to the Super Bowl. Parcells doesn't care about personalities. He cares about winning, and **he knows how to get that done.**

For months, the big rumor was about Parcells coming in to take over, but to me, that seemed too good to be true. I was figuring the Jets would find a way to screw it up. They didn't interview a soul after Rich Kotite left. Not one damn person, making it quite clear who they were waiting for. But just before the Super Bowl, NFL commissioner Paul Tagliabue stepped in and said Parcells couldn't coach anywhere else unless the Patriots agreed to it, and Patriots owner Bob Kraft said that was only happening if the Jets gave up the No. 1 pick overall in the 1997 draft *or* me, defensive end Hugh Douglas, and cornerback Aaron Glenn.

"Hey, Stacey, get me a plane ticket to New England," I

hollered at my agent's assistant that morning when I heard what Kraft said. "I'm getting traded."

I was kidding. Jerome Stanley, who also represents Douglas, was talking on his speakerphone to James "Shack" Harris, the Jets assistant general manager.

"There is **no way** we're going to trade Keyshawn, or Hugh, or Aaron," he said in his low, raspy voice. "You know that."

"Then why are their names out there?" Jerome asked.

"We can't control what the media does," Shack said. "And you know we can't control what Bob Kraft says. Heck, any owner or GM on any team in this country would have said the same thing, that they wanted Keyshawn, Hugh, and Aaron."

I wasn't worried. They weren't going to trade me. No way. I didn't think Hugh or Aaron were going, either. **Even the Jets aren't that stupid.** Hugh wasn't so sure, though. In fact, Hugh was in a frenzy, calling me, calling wide receiver Jeff Graham, calling all kinds of people to let them know he was pissed as hell.

"Damn the Jets," he said. "I can't believe they're talking about trading me."

I don't know why he was so upset. Everyone else on the team was *trying* to get traded.

Last season. **What a mess.** Someone asked Kotite at his departure press conference if the season had been a nightmare. He said no, but maybe he'd have nightmares later. Hell, who was he trying to fool? Every day was a nightmare for this team. Every game was like a bad dream.

I thought we were going to the playoffs, maybe even win the division. I was going to get 80 receptions, score 12 touchdowns, make big plays, win games. We weren't going to be laughed at. We weren't going to repeat what happened the season before, when the team won only three games.

I started last season as the No. 1 rookie wide receiver in the country. I finished it third in rookie receiving yards, behind Terry Glenn of the Pats and Eddie Kennison of the St. Louis Rams. I caught 63 passes for 844 yards and scored eight touchdowns, for which I was handsomely paid. All I know is those numbers should have been higher. So should have been the number of wins. **We won one lousy, stinking game.**

I knew one thing as we went through the season. It became very apparent what kind of coach we needed. Someone who knew how to lead. In this business, you've got to have a philosophy much like that of Miami's coach, Jimmy Johnson. Screw all your friends, the nice guys, and the great kids. Hire assistants who want to work, and get players who can play.

That was Kotite's problem. He hired his friends to be his assistants and *tried to make Wayne Chrebet into Jerry Rice.* Hell, we led the league in kids from Hofstra. Maybe the school gives the team a break on rent.

I don't know anything about the assistants Parcells brought in from the Patriots. From the Jets, they kept offensive line coach Bill Muir and tight ends coach Pat Hodgson, who is cool, but they let go wide receivers coach Richard Mann, which was wrong. Mann was the only one who had a clue last season, but nobody ever listened to him. Mann taught me a lot and made my entrance into the league a lot easier, especially after my holdout and all the shit I took (and dished out) the first couple of months with the team.

My big concern is that they also kept Ron Erhardt. And that should make this upcoming season very interesting, considering what I think of the man as an offensive coordinator, which you'll find out when you read this book. But I hope like hell he proves me wrong. I honestly hope he **shoves my words right back down my throat.** I want to win, and if that takes me being wrong about somebody— anybody—then so be it.

What we need to do now is clean up the roster. Get rid of all the Mahoneys just taking up space. Trade the No. 1 pick and get four or five good guys who can contribute right away. Or take Peyton Manning and let him battle for the starting job. We need a quarterback who isn't afraid to throw down the field, someone who just doesn't dump off four- and five-yard passes when we need seven for a first down. Someone who won't throw everything to the coach's pet. If we've got a guy worth $25 million, **it's time for him to step up.**

Looking over this book now, seeing what I wrote as it all unfolded, how I felt, what all went on, what we went through—damn, it's a wonder we're all not patients in some institution somewhere trying to figure out which way is up. It was a **crazy, miserable year.** And in the end—even though it hurt me not to be practicing for the playoffs—I was happy as hell to get home.

As my plane home from New York got close to L.A., I felt something huge being lifted right off my shoulders, and the dark cloud over my head starting to break up. As soon as we landed, I was heading straight to the apartment to see my girl and my daughter, Maia, who had just turned one. She's walking now.

My plan was to rest up for a while, then work out harder than ever. And I've been doing that. I'm coming back into camp faster, stronger, and with an attitude. Parcells, once he gets to know me, *is going to love me.* And if he doesn't? I'll just be Terry Glenn.

On the flight, I met a little boy who asked me for an autograph. I reached into my bag and pulled out one of my pictures that I had taken from my locker, and signed it for him. Once we landed in L.A. and were getting off the plane, he came up to me again and started tugging on my jacket.

"Are you guys going to be any better next year than you were this year?" he asked.

"Yeah," I answered, laughing, "if they get me the ball."

1 Negotiations

"No, Keyshawn Johnson is not here," I said softly to the voice on the other end of the phone and started to hang up. "For real, he's not."

When the phone rang in my New York City hotel room one August afternoon in 1996, I only had a guess as to who was doing the calling. Only a few people knew I was even in New York, so it should have been either one of my boys, my girl, or one of my agents giving me the word that I should either pack up and head back to Los Angeles, or that *my contract* with the "dog-ass" Jets was finally *done.* That's what the local paper had called my new team that morning in an article talking about my contract, or lack of one, and my two-week holdout. I kind of liked the term.

Absolutely nothing had gone according to plan since the Jets made me the first pick in the NFL draft in April, which is why I had **zero confidence** that the ringing phone was bringing me any kind of *good news.*

My agents and I had slid unnoticed into New York the night before and they had launched *a sneak attack* on the Jets that morning, arriving uninvited and unexpected at the Jets offices to try and get a contract done. They left me alone and it wasn't long before I got tired of sitting around in my hotel room. So for almost two hours I walked down Broadway in Manhattan, from the middle of the city down to someplace called the Village. I had never heard of it, but I walked there, trying not to be recognized because the Jets thought I was playing golf in Los Angeles. I don't even know how to play golf, but it seemed like a good thing for someone not in New York to be doing.

As I walked, I did a lot of thinking. The past months had taken their toll on me mentally and physically. I wasn't sleeping right. I wasn't eating right. I wasn't working out right. And mainly, I wasn't playing any ball. And here it was August 6. I made up my mind right there on Broadway that if my agents came back with even a little better money, I was signing the offer. I was tired of being a holdout, tired of sitting around, **tired** of listening to **nasty-ass negotiations** on a speakerphone. I was going to get my money, maybe it would have to be on the back end, when I became a free agent. Right then, I didn't care. I wanted to ball.

I had been back in my room about an hour when the phone started ringing. I thought it might be some nosy reporter who had spotted me. I had tried hard to stay invisible, but when you're **6' 4" with a one-carat diamond in one ear** and your picture's been on the cover of just about every sports section in America, it's a little difficult. People stared at me, figuring I must be somebody, but they couldn't get a fix on who. I told the bellman I was Everson Walls. I told the waiter at the Carnegie Deli that I was a freshman at USC, and I told the cab driver I was retired from the Raiders.

And now I was telling *some fool* that I wasn't me.

"No, Keyshawn Johnson is not here," I said into the

phone again. The receiver was halfway back on the cradle when I heard my agent, Jerome Stanley, shouting: "Key, Key! It's us and the Jets. Don't hang up!"

So I didn't. And suddenly they were all there on the other end. The good guys—my agents—and the bad guys, Jets president Steve Gutman and Pat Kirwan, director of player administration. They were telling me to come to camp. The deal was done. Finally. Time to play ball. For the **dog-ass Jets.**

That moment put the cap on some of the most stressful weeks of my life. I went from being the most **celebrated** college football player in America to being the most **unemployed** college football player in America. Most weeks I was strong, ready to fight, ready to stay out the entire season and go into next year's draft. And some weeks I just felt like signing anything to get this over with. I never wanted to be a holdout, but I was not about to be a fool.

The negotiation process really began in January 1996, when I came out publicly and said I wanted to play for the New York Jets. People reacted crazy. Nobody could believe I actually wanted to play for a team with a *sorry-ass history* and a 3–13 record in 1995.

But it made perfect sense to me. The Jets had the No. 1 pick and I was the best college player available. And then the Jets paid big money to get a quarterback, Neil O'Donnell, who had just led the Pittsburgh Steelers to the Super Bowl, and they beefed up the offensive line, getting Jumbo Elliott from the New York Giants. They also hired a new offensive coordinator, Ron Erhardt, who had run the show in Pittsburgh. But they all needed somebody who could take it in for six. *I figured it ought to be me.*

The Jets' scouts came to see me in the NFL combine in Indianapolis in February, a wacked process where players get measured and weighed and timed. I felt more like I was being ***prepped for a transplant*** than for pro football. They also saw me run with a group of my teammates at the University of Southern California during the spring. I ran a 4.41 that day over 40 yards, smoking everybody except some track dude who probably had never even seen a football. They also watched all my game films from USC and talked with just about every coach I'd ever had. Kirwan figured out that in my entire career at USC, I dropped a total of two balls. I think their minds were made up after that.

It wasn't long before they were calling my guys to try and work out some sort of pre-draft deal. I gladly would have signed a pre-draft deal if the money had been right. But the money wasn't right. **Wasn't even close.** The No. 1 pick in 1995, Ki-Jana Carter, got a deal with the Cincinnati Bengals that paid him $17 million over seven years with a $7 million signing bonus and an out-clause after four years, meaning he could up and leave or renegotiate. Simple logic said that all the Jets had to do was better that offer by 20% and I'm signed in a minute. Deal done. Let's play.

But the Jets didn't see it that way. Their first offer was for $16 million over seven years with a $6.3 million signing bonus spread out over three years. No out-clauses, no guarantees. Their reasoning for what they admitted was a

LOW OFFER was this: I was a wide receiver and wide receivers are generally not paid as high as running backs, which is what Carter is. Also—and here's the one I couldn't believe—that because I would be coming to New York, I would be in the largest media market in the country and therefore able to make up the difference in endorsement deals. It was the lamest line of reasoning I'd ever heard. Because I've got a **personality** and some **punch** behind it, I was being *penalized.*

It was like some baker getting a 9-to-5 at a bakery but getting paid below minimum wage because he sells pies out of his own kitchen at night. Made no sense to me. More than that, it wasn't fair. All I wanted was a fair deal.

But we had to play their game, so we countered with a proposal that would pay me a $7.3 million signing bonus and a six-year deal worth about $16 million. The Jets also said they wouldn't, under any circumstance, give me an out clause. The team had **NEVER** given a voidable to any player. In the past three drafts, players had sought and gotten voidables, and league owners were getting worried about the trend, basically because voidables mean that if the dude they pick isn't happy, the team has lost its investment. We knew Gutman wouldn't budge on the issue. He had been a member of the collective bargaining council that had dealt with this very issue and we knew that nobody understood it like he did. There was no point in trying to **TRICK HIM** with some sort of legal language. So we decided not to fight the voidable issue, figuring we give—now it's your turn.

This is where we stood heading into draft day, April 20. We were talking with Gutman and Kirwan every day leading into the final week, but nobody was budging on either side. It was fun to watch the media try to figure out what was going on. Gutman has a history of not commenting on negotiations and we weren't talking, but ESPN's Chris Mortensen thought he had it all figured out. He went on the air saying that talks between the Jets and me were stalled because I was insisting on a $10 million signing bonus and a contract worth $20 million. Mort was tripping.

Fred Edelstein, who publishes a newsletter named the "Edelstein Pro Football Insider," later would write that we had a pre-draft deal with the Jets. Edelstein was tripping, too. If we had a pre-draft deal, then why the hell were we fighting with the Jets at 9 a.m. the morning of the draft?

Although we didn't realize it at the time, a phone conversation the night before between Jerome and Gutman would set the tone for the months to come.

"You're screwing your client by not taking this offer," Gutman had said. I know spit was coming out the sides of his mouth.

"I'd be screwing my client if I did take this offer," Jerome said back.

"You're a fool if you don't take this deal. If you don't take this offer now, **we'll trade the pick,** you know that."

Fine, I said to myself while they argued some more. Trade the pick. I'd rather sign a deal for less money that was fair, that was structured differently, than sign this deal with the Jets. Trade me. I know I'm going to play wherever I go. Gutman won't have a job for long if he doesn't sign me.

The next morning, Kirwan sat with us and tried to play nice guy, reasonable guy. It wasn't working and the draft was only two hours away. He wasn't happy; neither were we. He got up to leave.

"What do I tell them?" he asked us. "How can I go back with this kind of counterproposal? You're asking for a hell of a lot of money."

"Tell them all we're asking for is a **fair deal.** It's a simple process," Jerome said.

Kirwan shrugged and was gone.

I asked Jerome if he thought the Jets were bluffing about trading the pick.

"I guess we'll find out."

They had to be bluffing, I was telling myself when I went back to my room to get dressed. **They need me** *a lot more than I need them.* Their owner, Leon Hess, the gas man, wasn't getting any younger and I knew that man wanted to win. I also knew they weren't going to the Super Bowl with Lawrence Phillips or Jonathan Ogden or Simeon Rice, the other top-rated draft picks. But they might with me.

I had finally reached the point where I said, **Screw it,** what happens happens. I was tired of thinking about it and tired of trying to figure out what somebody else was thinking and what they were going to do. This was the NFL draft and I was going to enjoy myself whatever the outcome. I didn't fly all these miles, pay for 16 of my friends and family members to fly all these miles, to spend the day **depressed.** Screw the Jets. This day was mine. I've been watching the draft on TV ever since they started televising it. Just like I had practiced signing my name for autographs as a little kid, I had envisioned myself up on that stage, cameras flashing, people cheering. Not even Gutman was going to wreck this day. This day was mine.

I did know one thing: Whatever happened, I was going to look good. ***My suit was as sweet as they come.*** I had met Ron Finley, a clothing designer with his own label, Dropdead Clothing, a while back in Los Angeles, and I'd asked him to come up with something for the draft. He hooked me up with a cream-colored, knee-length jacket and matching pants. I knew as soon as I slipped it on that morning that it was just right for a day like this. I gathered my crew and we got on the shuttle bus that would take us from the hotel to Madison Square Garden. I had my closest friends and family, people who have been with me from long, long ago. Everyone was dressed in their finest clothes and the women had cameras stashed in their purses. Everyone was **buzzing** with chatter and **bugging** the hell out of me, asking me what was going to happen and if I was nervous and all other kinds of bullshit. Right then I wished I'd brought my headphones.

I've been to Super Bowls and the NBA Finals, huge concerts and even riots. I've seen people crazed and excited, but there was nothing, nothing that compared to what I saw when I walked into the Paramount Theatre inside the Garden. When I got off the bus I saw a guy in green tights with a cape running around screaming. Another sane Jets fan. And all the way down the back hallway leading to the stage I heard my name echoing through the place. "Key-shawn John-son," "Key-shawn John-son." And when the fans saw me, the place blew up. I couldn't believe how loud they were and how green they were. I figured this wasn't the time to mingle. So I handed our daughter, Maia, to my girlfriend, Shikiri Hightower, grabbed my mother's hand, and headed backstage to be with the other guys who were also waiting to hear where their next home would be.

One by one we were called onto the stage to be introduced to the crowd. I walked out and ***the place went crazy again.*** I saw my crew standing in an aisle; the public relations people had told the families that once their guy got picked, they could run up onstage next to him to celebrate. My family was dead sure I was going first and they wanted to be ready.

Backstage the tension was thick. Guys fidgeting, standing up, pacing, trying to chatter at one another. A lot of **fake laughs** and **fake well wishes.** We weren't standing back there for each other. This was all about taking care of business for the rest of our individual lives. I kept looking up at a clock next to the bigscreen TV. This was taking forever.

Finally it was 11 a.m., and I watched the pre-draft ESPN stuff on the tube. Chris Berman was giving his predictions and then they flashed to a guy who was picking up a phone receiver from inside a green Jets helmet. He wrote something down and took it up to NFL commissioner Paul Tagliabue, who was waiting onstage to announce the No. 1 pick. And just then the phone next to me started ringing. It was Leon Hess, the 81-year-old owner of the Jets.

"Well, son. I guess we've got to go to the bank. You're our guy."

The television cameras caught my face as I broke into a huge smile while holding onto the receiver. And then I heard Tagliabue: "With the first pick in the 1996 draft, the New York Jets select wide receiver Keyshawn Johnson."

It was official. **I was the No. 1 pick.** The crowd erupted again, screaming, yelling crazy, waving banners and signs and jumping all over the place. I knew these folks wanted to win, but this was wild. I could barely hear Mr. Hess on the other end of the phone. I started to say something back when my agents started tugging on my sleeve, telling me that Tagliabue was waiting.

"Hey, *Tagliabue don't sign my paycheck*," I yelled at them. "Let me talk to the man."

And so I did. I told him he wouldn't be sorry, that I was going to do all I could to help him win games. He said that was all he wanted. And then I turned and walked out on stage with a Jets jersey in my hand. My family rushed up and I reached for my daughter, giving her a kiss that would be caught on the front page of *Newsday* the next morning. "Oh, Baby," it would say. Oh, baby, was right. After that it **was sheer insanity.**

I ran into the crowd and threw my hat to the fans. People were pushing me from one group of reporters to another.

"Welcome to New York," somebody was screaming as we made our way.

"Hey, Keyshawn, I want to have your baby," yelled another. I looked—it was a dude.

Finally we made it into the limousine that would take us out to Jets headquarters at Hofstra University on Long

Island. The fans swarmed the car, trying to stick papers, cards, footballs, all kinds of stuff through the window for me to sign. We took off, stopping to drop off my mother and sisters and the baby at the hotel. Traffic was keeping us from moving more than a few hundred feet at a time and when the driver said he couldn't turn left off of Broadway onto 44th, where our hotel was, I told him to pull over and we'd walk. I grabbed my baby and the diaper bag and headed with the group towards the hotel. People started **honking** and **screaming** when they saw me. I guess it was pretty funny to see a 6' 4" black dude in a knee-length suit holding a baby walking down a street in the middle of Manhattan. I felt like the mayor or something.

By the time we finally made it to the Jets training camp at Hofstra, a half-dozen TV cameras were waiting for me by the front door. So was Gutman, flashing what I'd begun to call his *smiley handshake* face. He led us up to his office, where Mr. Hess was waiting, nearly bouncing as we came in. He made a point of walking around the room introducing himself to each of my guys and my agents. The funny part came when Hess met my older brother Michael, who was outfitted in a high-necked pin-striped suit, one of those old-fashioned round hats, and tiny wire-rimmed sunglasses. Michael's always been on the cutting edge of fashion. But here was Mr. Hess, introducing himself to Mike like Mike was some **country club big shot.**

Hess didn't care what Mike looked like; Hess was cool. Hess was happy.

Smiley-faced Gutman walked me down to the office of

the wide receivers coach, Richard Mann. It happened to be his 49th birthday and he was sitting in a rocking chair, a Jets tradition for the position coach who caught that year's first draft choice. ***"Hey Richie, I got you a present,"*** Gutman said. Mann just smiled as I walked in the door. I didn't know it then, but Mann's help later on when I finally got to training camp would shape my entire season.

And then I caught a whiff of cigar smoke. **Kotite.** It had to be. It was. Head coach Richie Kotite slapped me on the back and shook my hand, looking tired but pretty happy. All the papers had said he would veto picking me because he was a blue-collar guy and I was all flash and dash.

But I think the bottom line was he wanted to win and I am a player. I guess he figured we'd find a way to co-exist. We'd see. I knew I'd be around for a while.

When the final press conference was finished and the last photo was shot, so was I. It had been an exhausting day. I was ready to get back to Los Angeles, but we couldn't make the last flight. So back in Manhattan we headed out to a restaurant, where my crazy family popped a few bottles of champagne and tried to make a big deal out of the day. I said no, not now, not tonight. Too much was running through my head. And even as I was falling asleep with Maia on my chest, happy that my dream of being drafted had been fulfilled, there were still a lot of troubling thoughts running through my head. By taking me, did the Jets think I'd eventually agree to their weak-ass terms? Or were they going to meet mine? I didn't know what they were thinking before the draft and I didn't know now. ***I was still a long way from the*** *money* and a *longer* *way from the playing field.*

Over the summer I tried not to think about contracts and negotiations and offers and deals. But it was tough. Especially because we weren't speaking with the Jets at all. Things broke off the week after the draft with neither side doing any moving on anything. The thought began to slip into my head that I might not be signed in time for rookie camp on July 13. It was a bad thought.

Mini-camp had been **a pain.** I played O.K., not great. But I was sick with the flu, had taken a red-eye flight the night before, and was still reeling from everything that had happened during the draft, just five days earlier. The DBs were hanging all over me, trying to show they could slow down the big man. Later I'd find out they said I was whining about the coverage. I had told them to keep their motherfucking hands off me. **That's not a whine. That's a threat.** I also heard that people thought the Jets' second round pick, Alex Van Dyke, had played better than me. He did. But we were in T-shirts and shorts. I didn't make All-America in T-shirts and shorts. Give me some pads and get me in a game.

The fatigue factor was mainly my fault. Two days after the draft I threw a little party. It was just about the baddest party Los Angeles had seen in some time. It started as Jerome's idea, but the more I thought about it, the more I got into the planning. We rented out the House of Blues in Hollywood for $25,000 and invited about 2,000 people. We also hooked up with Coolio, fresh off a

Grammy win for his song, "Gangsta's Paradise." By the time he took the stage, the place was popping. And when he started on his gangster song, **even the white people** were singing.

I spent most of the night running around trying to see everyone who had come. It was a crowd as diverse as Los Angeles itself. Movie stars Tori Spelling and Ice-T, athletes Lamont Warren from the Indianapolis Colts and Chris Mims from the San Diego Chargers—those two I had gone to high school with—and a late appearance by Deion Sanders. Security escorted us to a private room and we chilled for about half an hour, talking about everything from the league to women. With Deion, though, it's hard to tell whether what he gives you is genuine. I'm not sure whether I was with the *REAL Deion, or the one who PLAYS Deion on TV.*

The crowd was also filled with my friends' mothers, who used to feed me and let me sleep on their couches, women from Beverly Hills, women from South Central, and some of L.A.'s hardest-core, **inner-city gang bangers.** We also had a lot of security, not because we expected trouble with gangs—I have too much respect in the 'hood for that—but with numbers. My boys and I spent most of our younger years sneaking into parties like this one, so we knew all the tricks. A few years back I got into Magic Johnson's party by saying I was Chris Webber's brother. So we made sure every side door was guarded and everyone who stepped a foot inside had a valid invitation with the special stamp. I'd heard that *guys were trying to make copies at Kinko's.* We used to do that, too.

The people were cool. The only problem came when we started handing out party T-shirts. Some fools will do anything to get something for free. Even a weak-ass T-shirt. One of my guys onstage threw one to Mims but someone else tried to grab it and people started fighting. **SOME FOOL hit Chris in the head with a beer bottle** and he started to charge back, but thought better of it. Maybe he was envisioning the next day's headlines, which were sure to say something about an NFL star fighting at a Hollywood party. So the fight was over quickly, but it was enough to cut the party short and make the rounds around the league. I heard Bobby Beathard with the Chargers wasn't exactly thrilled with the news.

I don't think I got to bed until 6 a.m.; a bunch of us stayed in a hotel across the street from the club. The bad thing was that I had a class at eight and the badder thing was that I went. It was funny, but everybody just thought that I had quit school once we won the Rose Bowl back in January. But I only had to take three more classes to get my degree in History and **I always knew I'd get it done.** It was important to my mom and to my family; nobody else had ever gotten that far in school. I didn't want to be one of those stereotypical athletes who only cares about football and getting in the league. I've always been smart, just haven't applied myself at times. This was going to be different though. I was going to take something away from USC **besides a few MVP trophies.**

After graduation I spent a few days in New York, signing autographs at a card show and taking in a Mets game at Shea Stadium. Then it was time to start filming my Adidas commercial. They wanted four days of my time—two days on Astroturf somewhere in the San Fernando Valley, a day running steps at the Los Angeles Coliseum, and a day running on the sand in Malibu. That was fine with me because I needed the workouts. But I also needed things to be done right. Days in the Valley were reaching the $110°$ **mark** and the Coliseum wasn't a lot cooler. So I ordered two trailers, one for my family to hang out in and one with a bed so I could sleep during breaks. I also ordered special catering trucks, too. One day it was Mexican food from a local place I knew, the next it was South Central barbeque. The film crew was pumped, but gave me a lot of grief, saying I had gone too fast from the ghetto to Hollywood. **"Hey,"** I told them, "without me, you'd be **eating weak-ass sandwiches on dry bread."** Not surprisingly, by the end of the shoot, I was directing it, too.

The reporting date for rookies, July 13, came and went and *still no productive talks with the Jets.* In fact, we had talked very little. I wasn't really worried, but I wasn't happy, either. I had been working out a lot, spending mornings in the weight room at USC and afternoons at the track. A lot of guys who had made it in the league came back and we worked out together. Lamont Warren, the running back from Indianapolis, was one, and he brought Sam Rogers, who played for the Bills. Mims was around some, too. We pushed each other. It was good. But it wasn't camp.

Jets veterans reported July 19 and the media quickly jumped on the story of my holdout, *painting me as a* *greedy, cocky player* who didn't give a lick about the team. I had been warned about the media in New York, so I was prepared. But then it became the talk of the town and hour by hour I was getting killed. I had heard that most of the callers to WFAN, the local sports radio station, were pissed off at me and had started saying that I was trying to be like Shaquille O'Neal, who had just signed with the Lakers for $120 million. Things had really gotten **out of control.** We had to fight back.

On Monday, we set up a conference call with two of the Jets beat writers—Gerald Eskenazi from *The New York Times* and Paul Needell from the New York *Daily News*. Later I'd find out that the rest of the guys, Randy Lange from The Bergen County *Record*, Dave Hutchinson from The Newark *Star-Ledger*, and Mark Cannizzaro from the *New York Post*, were **angry as hell with us** for not including them. It didn't matter, because Needell and Eskenazi put us on a speaker phone so everybody could hear me anyway. Jerome was on the East Coast doing some work for another client and I had driven down to San Diego with my other agent, Lee Kolligian, and my buddy Skeats (Reynaldo Spalding, who plays at Portland State) to watch the Chargers practice. And that just pissed me off more, watching everybody else in camp except me.

On the phone, we made our position clear to the writers: **I was the No. 1 pick and I should be paid like the No. 1 pick. Not the sixth pick.**

We told them about the "endorsement logic" the Jets were using to justify their low-ball offer. Eskenazi asked if that was similar to Michael Jordan's situation where he was taking a low salary, until this year, because his off-court income was so extraordinarily high. I said, no, it wasn't like that at all. Jordan's done his thing, he deserves to get paid on both ends. His stuff is proven. Anything I'm doing off the field is based strictly on potential.

"I shouldn't be penalized for being the type of person I am, a happy kid, a kid who loves the game," I said.

They asked whether the holdout was taking its toll on me and whether I'd be able to make up what the other rookies had already learned.

"I'm not bitter. I'm frustrated because if you're going to take a guy No. 1, you should pay him No. 1. If they take me six, I have no problem taking what the No. 6 gets. If it takes me **24 hours seven days a week** to catch up, that's what I'll do. Right now I get up at nine o'clock, work out at 10. I'm running routes, catching the ball, lifting weights. I'm thick as leather. When I get on the field, I plan on earning all that I've gotten, giving people their money's worth.

"I'm not asking to break a record, put me on the cover of *Sports Illustrated* with money signs over my head saying, Big Deal. **If you take me one, pay me one,** it's all I'm asking. I want to go and play football."

It was, I thought, a simple conversation with a simple message, no funny stuff, no sneaky innuendo. I thought things were cool. But the next day the headlines in New York screamed:

KEYSHAWN RIPS JETS, SAYS HE'S NOT GETTING FAIR OFFER and KEYSHAWN RAPS JETS: CONTRACT TALKS TURN NASTY.

Now tell me how they get that from what I said? **Welcome to the New York animal, someone said.** And then I get ripped for talking, period. People were saying we screwed up because athletes just don't get involved in negotiations and should never talk to the press about them. Why the hell not? It's my contract. It's my future. Why shouldn't I be involved and why shouldn't I talk if I want to? Oh, they say, you'll anger your fellow teammates. They aren't going to be angry. It's not on them. They've all had contract problems one way or another. Why should they care about my business anyway? Just because something has always been done a certain way does not make it right. Nor does it mean I have to do it that way, too. People are going to have to realize that I do things because **that's who I am** and **what I believe in.** I am an individual and because of where I've been and what I've seen, that's who I am. I couldn't care less if anyone likes it or not.

Jerome went on WFAN with sports analyst Mike Francesa. I know **Francesa's face was turning red** when he started screaming at Jerome on the air, saying: "This will backfire on you with the fans, I'll tell you that. It's going to hurt your kid if you don't get him signed. This team has no reputation of being cheap with its players."

"That's why I don't understand why they're doing it now," Jerome said.

"Hey, all I know, it's going to hurt your kid if you don't get him signed."

Later, as we were sitting in Jerome's office trying to sort this whole thing out, Jerome grimaced: "This is a real sick game."

I was sick of being a player in this game. What was worrying me was that the Jets were starting to prepare to play without me. The day of our conference call they signed two wide receivers: little-known Elbert Ellis, a 6' 5" kid with world-class speed but no hands, and veteran Webster Slaughter, who had been coached by Richard Mann before. Even though Webster's an old dude, he can still play. I decided things were looking bad. They even decided to give Wayne Chrebet, another receiver, a three-year contract. I told myself that if there was no movement by the end of the week, I was going to **demand a trade.** And at week's end, when Jerome, Gutman, and I got on a conference call together, I dug in. I told him there was no way I'd ever play for the Jets for this kind of money. Ever.

And then Jerome started calling other teams. I flew up to Oakland on Thursday, July 25, to see Shikiri and Maia, who were staying with Shikiri's parents in Berkeley. The morning I got in, I went over to Cal and worked out with some of the guys I knew there, and then I went to watch the Raiders practice. I talked with some folks there, too. They had to be careful because of the tampering rule and all that, but I let them know that **I'd love to be playing for the Raiders.** I'd be on the West Coast, which would solve a lot of problems for me. I'd be closer to Maia and to my mom, for whom I had just bought a $1.3 million house in the Los Angeles suburbs. Football season is tough enough on families when you're nearby, and being halfway across the country can only make it tougher.

Jerome talked with a couple of teams about trying to work out some sort of trade. The teams were interested and I was ready. But when we talked to Gutman again, and said we wanted him to trade me, he said there was **absolutely no way** they were going to do that. I flew back to Los Angeles late Sunday night, confused and upset.

One twist to the whole negotiations had to do with the deal the Baltimore Ravens gave offensive tackle Jonathan Ogden. His agent, Marvin Demoff, asked for a seven-year deal worth $17 million with an out-clause and a $7 million signing bonus. And team owner Art Modell simply said, O.K. Modell didn't want the public relations nightmare of having a holdout the same year the team was trying to endear itself to a new city.

Ogden's deal screwed up everything because he was the fourth pick. I was the No. 1 pick and I was sup-posed to get the best deal, which made it impossible for us to get less than Ogden; the Jets were being forced to pay more because of Modell's image problems. I think that probably set us back a couple of weeks.

Early Monday morning Jerome and I sent a revised proposal to the team, a proposal that we thought was a **fair compromise.** I was asleep on the couch when the Jets called back at three o'clock. On their end was James "Shack" Harris, one of the Jets' executives, and Kirwan. I had a feeling, however, that Gutman wasn't far off.

"We got your latest proposal," Shack said.

"So we got a deal?" asked Jerome.

"Heh, heh, heh," came the booming bass chuckle over the speakerphone.

Shack's got a laugh like Barry White. And we heard it a lot during negotiations. He kept things moving and he kept things from exploding. He's probably the biggest reason why I didn't come out of this thing totally *hating* the organization.

He told us the sticking point in our proposal was basically twofold. They didn't like the structure of the bonus and they didn't like the incentives we had suggested. We were now asking for a $6.75 million signing bonus and a six-year deal worth $16 million. We wanted the bonus up front; they wanted to defer much of it to the end of the contract so as to keep me from demanding a renegotiation later in the deal. To us, the first-year figures were important in that the money was the only guarantee I'd get because the organization, we were told, never gives guarantees. It also made sense for me tax-wise. Right then I was a resident of Las Vegas, where my corporation, Keyshawn Inc., is located. But once I started spending half the year in New York, I would become a New York resident and subject to all its **ridiculous taxes.**

We agreed to move part of the money back, but not as much as they wanted. We weren't budging from that, so they moved to the incentives. The way we worked it, if I reached two of the four "trigger" points in any two years I'd get an extra half-million dollars. If I did it in any three years, then I'd get an *additional million.* We proposed the triggers be 85 catches, 1,000 yards receiving, 35% of play, and six wins.

"Those seem a little low. You know you'll be playing

more than 35 percent. That's why we drafted you," Shack said. "And the 1,000 yards ... "

"Hey," I said. ***"How many receivers in Pittsburgh caught more than 1,000 yards*** with O'Donnell and Erhardt running the show?"

"Well, one," Shack said. "But how many the year before?"

"None. Zip. It's not easy. They play a five-receiver set."

"Keyshawn, you're going to get your passes and your yards. That's why we drafted you No. 1."

"And that's why we added six wins to the structure," Jerome interjected.

"Well, if we don't win more than six games this year we're all going to be gone anyway," said Shack. "What about making the Pro Bowl the third trigger instead of the 35 percent?"

"Twenty-three guys caught 1,000 yards last year and all of them didn't make the Pro Bowl," I argued.

"But you're better than *ALL* of them," Shack insisted.

"Then get me into camp," I shouted.

The next day's talks were no better. What was it going to take? Even Lawrence Phillips was now in camp, having signed the **worst deal** in the history of the NFL, a three-year contract with the St. Louis Rams with no signing bonus. And he was the sixth pick. If he can get into camp, what the hell was I doing still working out at USC?

The talk started circulating around Los Angeles that the trouble was because of my two agents. Ever since I hired them I'd been hearing nothing but bad things from other people. Talk about sick games. **The agent game is the sickest.** I had agents crawling all over me from the time I first set foot on the USC campus. And that was in January 1994. Before I'd even had a first practice. Everybody either was an agent himself or had a guy he wanted to fix me up with. Even our athletic director, Mike Garrett, former Heisman Trophy winner and all that—he had a guy he wanted me to talk to. I said no to everyone. Even Garrett.

After my last day of college eligibility, the 1996 Rose Bowl, I set up private interviews with the agents I liked the best and respected the most. In the end I chose Lee Kolligian because he had experience in doing marketing for Muhammad Ali; also, he had given two of my guys jobs as runners and it was a way of helping them out, too. Loyalty goes far with me. Lee got a law degree from Stanford and came from a very rich family that has handled its money well. I liked him. And I hired Jerome Stanley because Jerome and I grew up much the same. Like me, he went to Dorsey High School, West Los Angeles (junior) College, and USC. *He's walked the same road as I have and he* understands *what I'm about.* He's also been in some heavy contract talks before, dealing with the Boston Celtics for his clients Brian Shaw (now with the Orlando Magic) and Reggie Lewis, who passed away in 1993. Jerome can be a **hard-ass** and a lot of people don't like him. That's because he gets business done and doesn't really care whether he comes out of it with people liking him. I know that people also don't like him *because he's black.* It's a fact of life. But I didn't choose Jerome because he was black, just as I didn't choose Lee because he is white. They were the best representatives for me. Period. End of story.

I wondered whether agent Leigh Steinberg was behind a lot of the talk about Jerome and Lee and all the speculation about why my deal wasn't done. I didn't expect that from him; *I THOUGHT HE WAS A LOT CLASSIER.* But I had heard the stuff he was saying and it wasn't good. I guess Leigh was just mad he didn't get me. Oh, he tried. He contacted me through a runner during my senior season and tried to set up a couple of meetings. I didn't appreciate Steinberg's back-door approach so I blew him off. When I narrowed my choices to four, Steinberg wasn't on the short list. He wasn't happy to find that out. He tried to **weasel his way in,** calling a friend to say he was still interested, but in the same breath said I was making a huge mistake by not hiring him. I think he was just ticked that I was breaking his streak of representing the top pick in the last 10 drafts. And I was right in his backyard. It did occur to me that Steinberg was the agent for O'Donnell, who, eventually, was going to have to throw me the ball. I just hoped that O'Donnell cared more about **winning** than he did about **politics.**

By Friday, August 2, things had reached a dead end. The Jets had made no concessions and were trying to pressure me, saying I was risking all my endorsements and hurting my team. They even called on the afternoon I was seeing my new Adidas commercial for the first time. Shack

Harris was on the phone saying some of my teammates wanted to talk to me.

"Who?" I said. They didn't know it but I'd been talking with several of the guys—Hugh Douglas mainly—all along.

"Nick Lowery," Harris said. I handed the phone to Jerome and shook my head.

"Nick Lowery is 50 years old. I am never, ever going to be on the field the same time as Nick Lowery. I am never going to be in a huddle with Nick Lowery. At least they could have gotten O'Donnell."

I spent the next two days *depressed,* watching everybody else balling in the preseason. I felt worse and worse. Sunday afternoon, Jerome called and said it was time to make things happen. I was right with him.

"Get packed," he said. "We're going to New York."

Jerome's rationale was that because of the potential success of my career, especially off the field, we could not afford to jeopardize its start. He believed that it was smart to make the best deal at the best time, smarter than making a slightly better deal at the wrong time. My situation had gotten to the point where only slight gains would be made, if that, if I kept holding out. Jerome said that although the slight gains might help the perception of the contract within the "agent" community, and help him recruit other athletes in the future, the risk of holding out for these gains was not in my best interest. Mainly because I, *unlike other recent high draft picks, already have some pretty fly* off-the-field endorsement contracts.

I had the shoe thing going on with Adidas and a clothing line that would come out within a year; I had a trading card deal, an Internet deal with SportsLine, a deal with Oakley sunglasses, and this book. We needed to get me signed.

So that was how I found myself in a New York City hotel room, answering a telephone call with the voice on the other end telling me that I'd be heading to camp to sign a six-year deal worth $15 million, with a $6.5 million signing bonus and another $2 million up for grabs in incentives.

That morning, Jerome had decided that he and Lee would show up on the team's doorstep first thing and **force** the negotiations into **make-or-break mode.** I wanted to be there, but they wanted to use me as leverage if things got close: Do-this-deal-and-we'll-have-him-here-in-an-hour type stuff.

So as I was walking in the middle of Manhattan, Jerome and Lee were asking for Gutman at the Jets front desk. They said *the receptionist turned pale* as she heard their names and frantically started trying to find someone—anyone—to come downstairs to get them. Gutman was in Manhattan and Kirwan was on the practice field. Finally, Shack Harris appeared and took them to lunch while the Jets regrouped.

The funny part of the whole day was that while Jerome and Lee were upstairs, reporters a level below were calling their offices in Los Angeles for updates. Jerome had told them the night before that talks were off and that he was heading to Europe in a few days. They were mad when they found out the truth. We saw the payback a few days later when they blistered Jerome and me.

In the end, we gave, the Jets gave. Even though the papers would say we caved and the Jets won, we came out with more money than they had originally offered and a deal that gave me **the highest** per-year average for any rookie in NFL history. I was going to be **happy** for a **long, long time,** and so was my family.

But I knew none of this as I headed in a cab back to the hotel from my walk down to the Village. We passed a Hess gas station and I yelled out the window, "Sell more gas." The cab driver started to laugh.

"You play for the Jets?" he asked.

"Nope."

"You look like a ballplayer."

"I'm retired, from the Raiders. You like the Jets?"

"Oh yeah," the driver said. "I'm a huge fan. The biggest. I know everything about that team. Everything."

"How about that new head coach, the black guy?"

"Oh, no, you're thinking of Ray Rhodes, he's in Philadelphia. The Jets got Kotite, second-year man."

"They still got Boomer?"

"Oh, no. Boomer's gone. Arizona, I think. They got O'Donnell now, you know, from the Steelers. Played in the Super Bowl last year. Hell of an arm. Needs some help though. **The Jets sucked last year.**"

"Who'd they draft anyway?"

"Oh, I don't know. A couple of guys I never heard of."

I just sat back and laughed to myself.

Preseason

I'm living pretty large now, but it wasn't always like that. Believe me.

Nobody in Los Angeles or New York, or anywhere for that matter, knows this, knows how things were for me growing up. *All people see is the MONEY* I've got now and the things I've bought. But back when I was a kid, my mother, Vivian Jessie, and I hit some hard times. For a while we lived on the streets. For real. I spent my 11th birthday at the Venice Beach Homeless Shelter. I remember it because I used to take care of the little kids in daycare for some pocket change and they threw me a little party and gave me a plaque. **For a while, we even lived in a car.** We had moved to the shelter in Compton and a lady my mom made friends with gave us this beat-up, old blue Chevy that she didn't need anymore. It became home.

I was the youngest of my mom's six kids. The first five have the same father. But he took off and my mother started hanging out with the brother of one of her friends. When she got pregnant with me, her mother urged her to go with my dad to Iowa, where he was living most of the time. But she wouldn't leave her other children and she didn't want to burden a young man with six kids. So she stayed and he left. I never met the guy, but I hear I look just like him. Somewhere in Los Angeles I have more half-brothers and sisters, kids he fathered along the way. I didn't want to know the guy back then and ***I SURE AS HELL don't need him now, wherever he is.***

With six kids you don't work. So my mom raised us with welfare money. Sometimes the older ones would go live with other relatives and friends. But it was always me and my mom. I didn't want to go anywhere else. For a while we were living in my grandmother's house near downtown Los Angeles. When she passed, my mother and her brother had a big falling-out. The next thing I knew, we were out of the house. ***I never have understood why,*** and my mother doesn't talk much about it now. I knew it hurt her, and I made a vow then that I was going to make some money in my life and buy her that house back. She always said she didn't want that raggedy-old house back. But I know she did.

Once we got the car, life got a little simpler. My mom would drive me to school every morning, then pick me up over at USC, where I'd hang out every afternoon with the football team. John Robinson was the coach then and he sort of adopted a bunch of us who lived around the neighborhood. He'd let us hang out on the field, where we'd watch practice and then beg the players to let us carry their helmets or pads or whatever back to the locker room. I got real close to Marcus Allen, Ronnie Lott, Tim Shannon—a bunch of guys who, to me, were **true heroes.** I wanted to be just like them. Sometimes they'd take us out and buy us some food, but the real treat was when they'd take us to the dining hall where all the players on the team ate dinner. Most times that was the only meal I'd eat all day. I'd always grab a little extra and ask them to wrap it up so that I could take it to my mom.

She'd pick me up from USC and we'd drive somewhere to park and spend the night. Sometimes it was in the parking lot of a friend's apartment complex, but most often it was in the parking lot of the mortuary. It was safe there, she said. **Nobody shoots up a mortuary parking lot.**

Once a week, we'd check into a cheap motel where we could take showers and wash our clothes out in the sink. None of my friends knew we were living like this. I wasn't ashamed, we were doing the best we could. It just wasn't anyone's business. She'd pick me up and I'd jump in the back and put the blanket over my head so that nobody would see me.

Eventually, though, it got to be too tough and dangerous to live in the car. The neighborhood had always been ruled by drug dealers, and now the gangs were filling up and starting wars all over the place. **Drive-bys** became the way **gang bangers** could prove themselves. It got pretty crazy. After one night when we heard a lot of gunfire, I finally convinced my mother to let me start "working" with my brother Mike, who was living with some cousins and making a bunch of money scalping tickets.

Mike's always been a man of action and he had a pretty good system in place. It started when he made friends with some of the Dodgers players by hanging out around the ballpark. Mike Marshall was one of the players. He'd leave us four tickets at will-call, *we'd pick them up and then sell them.*

I was about 12 by then, no older, and standing outside the stadium with all the old guys, making some money. Sometimes the cops would confiscate tickets from the old guys and give them to us to sell because they knew we needed the money.

When we couldn't get tickets from Marshall or somebody else, we'd do what the other scalpers did, buy a group of tickets at a low price and then turn around and sell them for more. We'd figure out when Fernando Valenzuela was going to pitch, and then go scoop up a bunch of $3 seats in advance and sell them game night for $10 or $15 a pop because the game was sold-out.

When baseball season ended we turned to football. Back then the colleges would actually hand out tickets to the players to give to their families or friends. I'd get a couple from one guy and then I'd hit up the coaches one by one so ***nobody really knew*** how many tickets I had. The price depended on what game, who was playing. We'd work the college games on Saturday and the Raiders games on Sunday. And in between seasons we'd work the World Wrestling Federation events, buying 50 or so seats well in advance. We started to make a good deal of money, enough that my mom and I were able to find a place to live near USC and pay some bills. ***I was 12 YEARS OLD and supporting my family.*** I grew up fast. Real fast. But later things would turn pretty ugly, and I had to grow up all over again.

A lot of this was racing through my mind as I rode out to Jets camp on Long Island on August 6, just after I'd found out that my deal was done. I had come a long way. I knew that. And now I was finally getting a chance to play some real football. I started thinking about the new problems I was going to face once I got to camp. I'd missed 24 days of workouts with the team and virtually all of the two-a-days. I was coming in amidst a lot of publicity, good and bad. And I wasn't sure how it was going to play. I knew there'd be some jealousy and a lot of talk. Maybe some guys would try sweating me. I'd have to set that straight real fast, I said. Anybody sweating me was going to have trouble, period. Deal with who I am and what I've got. **I was here to play football and help this team win games.** That was all anyone needed to be concerned about. If I didn't produce, then it was on me.

About the last thing I thought, though, was that getting a chance to produce was going to be such a problem. I had no idea how frustrating and agonizing the next few weeks would be. That my everyday mantra would be, *"They've got to get me the ball.* **Just give me the damn ball!"**

My first day of practice was really nothing, although you'd never know it by the number of fans and media who turned out to watch. We had a preseason game the next night against Philadelphia so practice was just a walk-through of plays we were planning to run. I had been messing with Kotite since I got there to let me play in the game, but he wouldn't go for it, so I just stood on the sidelines. I had caught a couple of soft passes during warmups, hearing the soft whir of about a dozen camera motor drives. Good thing I didn't drop anything—even a soft pass. I could see the next day's story: **JOHNSON A BUST IN FIRST PRACTICE.**

I could, for the most part, follow what plays the offense was running. Nobody knew this, but Richard Mann, the wide receivers coach, and I had talked just about every week throughout the summer and during my holdout. I had diagrammed a lot of what was already in the playbook. When I got my legitimate copy after meetings that first night, I was up until about 4 a.m., reading through it and trying to learn whatever I could. My plan all along was to work as hard as I could to make up for the time I had missed. I knew it would hurt me at first. I knew I'd be running the wrong way sometimes, screwing a few things up. But the bottom line was *this was* **football,** *not* **brain surgery,** and football is something I know inside and out. John Robinson ran a pro-style offense at USC and from what I could tell, the system the Jets used was not that much different. Just the terminology. For example, at USC we called a little turn upfield a pivot move. The Jets call it a delay. USC uses the word option, the Jets call it a read.

The strange part was not knowing all the little, unwritten things about the team: where to line up for stretching; what time you were supposed to be heading out the door to practice; what time you were expected to lift weights or watch film. I knew the bus for Philly was leaving at 4 p.m. and **I didn't want to screw that up** my first day. So I was packed, ready, and waiting by 3:30, then sat outside until I saw other guys getting on. I knew I'd be straight soon.

But what I wasn't having was any talk about rookie rituals. There was noise the first night about making me sing. I told them flat out, I'm not singing. **Yeah, I'm a rookie,** *but I'm a grown man and I didn't come to this team to* **sing.** I wouldn't have asked any of them to run in front of a bus. I don't sing. Period. Then there was talk about tying me to a goal post. I killed that one fast, too.

"Anyone lays a motherfucking hand on me, they'd wish they didn't," I said.

They thought I was joking.

"I ain't joking. Try me."

Then it was, **"Damn, he's serious."** There was a little resentment about that from the other young guys who I'm sure had gone along with all that bullshit. The veterans didn't seem too happy, either. But I didn't care. I would show my team loyalty in the huddle and in the end zone. I didn't need to be doing nothing else.

The other issue I had to take care of quickly was the trash-talking. Now, I'm all for using your mouth in the intimidation war, but *rule No. 1 in trash-talking is you* ***DON'T*** *do it to your own* ***TEAMMATES.***

You save it for the bad guys on game day. But right off, the first day in pads and number 23, Melvin Crawford, was breaking my rules. I had gone long for a pass and Crawford, a third-team defensive back who was trying to make the team, did a pretty good job defending against me. But as we ran back to the huddle he started in on how he was showing me a thing or two, rubbing the play right in my face. I about punched him out. But instead I stopped him on the field and pulled his jersey.

"You'd better shut your mouth before my fist goes down your throat," I said real quietly. "You don't jump up and down until you make this fucking team. One play don't make a superhero."

And it doesn't break one, either. The guy got my point. He didn't say a word the rest of camp. He didn't make the team, either.

I was having problems with a couple of other players, too. One was Wayne Chrebet, the little wide receiver from Hofstra who Kotite was in love with. The kid does have guts—he came from nowhere and fought his way onto the team—but eventually he was going to have to step aside. *You **DON'T** pick someone No. 1 and pay him all that money to back up some dude,* no matter how much the coach likes that dude.

Just about every day after practice Kotite was praising me for working hard but defending Chrebet to the media, like he was afraid the kid would fade away with the spotlight on me. He'd say things like, "Once every 10 or 15 years you get a player like Wayne Chrebet who gives you everything." Well, Wayne Chrebet got you three wins last season.

Everyone was thinking the rivalry was going to be between me and Alex Van Dyke, the wide receiver the Jets drafted in the second round. Van Dyke is cool. He was learning, just like me. But Chrebet had an attitude. First time I walked into a wide receivers meeting, I sat down in a chair that, I guess, was Chrebet's, only because he had been sitting there every day since camp started. He came up and said, **"You're in my seat."**

"What?" I asked.

"You're in my seat."

"Fine, I'll move," I answered as he glared at me. "I know I'm going to be playing no matter where I sit." *I didn't think we'd be hanging out much.*

I couldn't believe the number of fans who came out to watch us practice. Every day there were about a thousand people crammed along the sidelines, screaming and yelling like it was the Super Bowl. These people were crazy. We had fans at USC practice, but not geared out in team colors and going wild on every play. Anything I did, they were cheering and chanting. It was cool, especially when they'd throw to me in the end zone. Even I got up about that.

The first day in pads my calves cramped up. I'd never had a cramp before so I didn't know what was going on at first. *I just knew my legs HURT LIKE HELL.* I doubled over and dropped to the grass. I swear the place went silent as the trainers sprinted across the field. And when I stood up and started walking it off, it was like I was Kirk Gibson in the World Series. Reporters started calling it, **"CRAMPS HEARD 'ROUND THE WORLD."** It was funny, but I could hardly walk the next day.

By the New York Giants preseason game on September 17 I was feeling pretty good about what I'd learned so far. I was working my butt off night and day trying to stuff it all in my head. I was up by 6:30 a.m. every morning and in Coach Mann's office by seven watching film.

It became a sort of ritual. We'd sit in there for a couple of hours until the first team meetings. All the other coaches were nosy, wondering what we were talking about, trying to peer inside. Mann got fed up after a while and shut the door and pulled the shades. His patience with me was real cool. *He's as dedicated to this game as* **any** *coach I've had.* I knew that if I hadn't held out, things would have been a lot different. I'd have been working out with the first team, getting all the reps, all the passes. I really didn't think I'd be full strength until the second or third game of the season. I'd gotten the plays down, I thought, but it was the physical aspect, getting myself into game shape, that was going to take a bit longer.

It wasn't long before people started asking me about whether I felt pressured heading into my first game. Pressure to play, to catch the ball, to score. People just don't realize they can't squeeze me. **PRESSURE** is growing up in South Central Los Angeles with *a gun to your head. This is* **NOT** *pressure.* This is football. Everybody wants you to think it's so much harder. People wanted to know if I was taking the team to the playoffs, to the Super Bowl this year. **Hey, I am no savior.** I am one man on a team with a sorry recent history. Somebody asked me if I was the black Joe Namath. That was funny. I told the dude I didn't even know who Joe Namath was. I didn't tell that to Joe, though, when he came to camp a couple of days before our preseason game against the Giants. Joe's cool.

Probably the best thing about getting ready for the Giants was breaking camp. Living in the dorms at Hofstra was killing me. The beds were too short, the air conditioning was blasting, I was freezing at night, and my phone bill was nearing the thousand-dollar mark. I couldn't wait to get out and get with my girlfriend, Shikiri, and our daughter, Maia, who flew in the night we broke. And I had only been in camp a week. I was already dreading next year. I understood the philosophy of training camp, building team unity, all that. But I couldn't see what purpose having us living in dorms and sleeping on hard beds for three weeks served. I knew we'd all be a lot happier sleeping in our own beds.

By the time the game came, I was dying to get on the field, to show why they were paying me all this money. But things didn't go as planned. First, I got lost driving to Giants Stadium and had to stop twice and ask gas station guys how to get there. They looked pretty surprised to see me. And I had been told I'd play a lot in the game, but in actuality, I played only one down in the first half. That really pissed me off. They didn't pick me to sit on the sidelines. My first catch didn't come until our backup quarterback, Frank Reich, found me for nine yards midway through the third quarter. I caught another pass for six. Frank overthrew me once and underthrew me two times, one of which was picked off.

I was angry I didn't play more, but oh, well. I was frustrated, yeah, but glad the first game was over and that I didn't screw anything up. I had to admit it felt pretty cool walking into the stadium and onto an NFL field, playing alongside players I'd been watching every Sunday. "Did I look big out there?" I asked a buddy of mine, Tamecus Peoples, who lives with me and runs my charity foundation.

"Towering," he said.

That's why I pay him.

The day after the game brought about the worst thing I've ever seen in football. Cut day. ***Damn, it's a cold process.*** It really made me stop and think about how lucky I am, and be thankful for all that I've got. Guys are just tapped and told to turn in their playbooks. Just like that. Guys who had dreams just like mine and abilities to play. **Cut. Boom. Gone.** Some of these guys had families, too. Now they've got to go back to wherever and get a 9-to-5. Damn. Some of these guys could play, too. Chris Hayes was one. He grew up in Los Angeles and played for Washington State. The Jets made him their 7th-round draft pick—a longshot to make the team, for sure—but the guy could play. He wasn't any worse than anyone else. He brought his girlfriend and their year-old baby to camp, holing up in the Long Island Marriott. His future was hanging on making the team. And he got cut. Damn. I'm going to retire before I ever get cut.

Practices were becoming a problem. I was improving every day—everyone kept saying that—but it was becoming really obvious that ***nobody wanted to get me the ball.*** A lot of times, the quarterbacks—Neil O'Donnell and Frank Reich—weren't even looking my way. I had no idea that I was going to have to lobby, sell myself, once I got to the pros.

I started to get real tired of our offensive coordinator,

Ron Erhardt, too. He was in my ear at every practice from minute one until the end, saying, You this, you that. Barking, chattering, talking way too much. That just doesn't work with me. Finally, it got so bad one day that I stopped dead in my tracks and decided I'd had enough. **"Shut up and just let me play,"** I yelled at him.

"You are just dumb, plain dumb," he yelled back. "Study the damn playbook."

That really set me off. All I'd been doing was studying the playbook. And dumb? I was not about to take that kind of **verbal abuse** from any coach, I didn't care who he was. These coaches had to learn how to talk to me. They didn't need to make it seem like I didn't know what I was doing out there and then praise some guy who catches a pass for eight yards, who didn't shake or lose nobody.

Sitting up in their glass-enclosed perch overlooking the field, Shack Harris and Pat Kirwan saw me and Erhardt going at it. They came running down to the field and tried to get me to calm down so that the reporters wouldn't get wind of what was happening.

"I'm not calming down for nobody," I told them. "You just don't talk to players like that. If I need to be corrected, correct me when we're watching the films. Or talk to me like a man, not some damned monkey."

I went home that night angry and confused.

And I started to wonder whether racism was a player on this team.

I know it exists—it exists everywhere—and I had to ask myself whether decisions made on this team became, at some point, **black-white issues.** They got rid of Brad Baxter, a brother who could play. And they got rid of Jeff Sydner, another brother with moves and who *was* running back punts. They moved Chrebet to punt-return duties, something I'll never understand. Chrebet may be gritty, but he's not going to be busting any punt returns. Not against NFL special teams squads filled with hungry men.

And I'd heard that **Kotite loved Jim McMahon** and hated Randall Cunningham. He loves Chrebet. I'm not ready to say that anybody on this team is racist or that any decision made was based only on skin color, but I have to be honest, **I did wonder.** Maybe that's just my upbringing. You don't go through life as a young black man in Los Angeles without experiencing that shit on some sort of level.

I felt it when I was a kid, watching all the white kids on the other sideline with good equipment, and I felt it when I got pulled over by the police for no other reason than being in the "wrong" neighborhood in the wrong kind of car. But that's an **everyday occurrence** for black men in L.A. Hell, it happened to me twice over the summer—even after I'd been the USC hero and my face had been plastered on newspapers and magazines all over the country.

I was driving down Sunset Boulevard during the middle of the day and I got pulled over for changing lanes without using my signal. There were zillions of cars on Sunset, but the police decide to pull over the brother in the metallic-blue, $100,000 Porsche. For failing to signal.

"You've been paying that much attention to me changing my lanes?" I asked the two white officers who came up to my car when I pulled over.

He said, Yes this, yes that. I just looked back at him and shook my head.

"You know what this is?" I asked him. "This is you having a problem because I'm a black man driving **this car** in **this part of town.** If you're writing me a ticket for failing to signal when I change lanes, then that says to me that you've got a problem with the car I'm driving and me in it."

He wrote the ticket. I paid the fine.

A week later, I was driving down Wilshire Boulevard to a friend's house when the police flashed their high beams on me from behind.

"Oh, no," I said to myself. "Here we go again."

I pulled over and rolled down my window and asked the man why.

"WELL, YOU'RE GIVING US THAT ATTITUDE."

"That attitude? I wasn't speeding. I wasn't driving reckless. I was even using my damned turn signal. Why did you pull me over?"

The cop got flustered.

"Well, you've got that tassel hanging from your rearview mirror and it's obstructing your view."

I glared at the guy, stunned at what I was hearing.

"Man, you should be happy I got that tassel. That's from graduating from USC. I went to college and I graduated from college and I can see just fine through my windshield. You can't see beyond my car and the color of my skin. Buddy, it's your view that's messed up."

He wrote the ticket. I paid the fine. **RACISM is a**

CANCER that is threatening to destroy this society. It exists on the streets, It exists in the big corporations, and *It exists in the NFL.*

I wonder whether it existed on my team, and, if so, was it showing itself? Maybe it had nothing to do with Kotite or Erhardt. I was thinking about all this the night after Erhardt and I had the first of what would be a million fights during practice. What was it going to take to make things right with this team? **What was it going to take** for them to find out what kind of player I really was and what I could do? It was hard to sleep.

And then it was time for our last preseason game. We were playing the Raiders at Oakland, and I was geared up to play against the team I'd love to be playing for and the team I grew up watching. I made my first $5 by watching a rich white dude's car while he went to the game at the Los Angeles Coliseum. That's when we lived across the street. Now the team was back up north, but my family was piling into cars and making the 10-hour drive to see me play in person.

There was **some strange shit** going on with this game. I'd heard that somebody had put a bounty on my head. Somebody wanted me hurt and out of the game and maybe out for the season. What I'd heard was that it started with a player on the Kansas City Chiefs squad. This guy was supposedly paying somebody on the Raiders $150,000 to take me out. Apparently there were some players in the league who weren't real happy about my entrance. They **didn't like my mouth** and most likely weren't real happy with the Porsche, the diamond-studded Rolex, my endorsement contracts, my own shoe with Adidas, my own commercial, and my own book. And they probably didn't like that I held out for more money. I didn't like it either, but I wasn't calling for nobody's head.

I really didn't take the bounty seriously. Actually, it was kind of funny. Because if somebody was going to take me out, then our coaches were going to have to **break down and actually call a play** to get me the ball.

Second, somebody on the Raiders would then have to catch me. And then we'd see who would do any taking of anybody out. I guarantee I'd still be standing. Anyway, it turned out there was nothing to the rumors.

The good news was that I'd been told I'd be playing almost the entire game. Not starting—that would be way too radical—but playing a lot. The bad news was that Neil O'Donnell wasn't going to play at all. They said that Frank Reich, the backup, needed the work. Hell, Neil needed the work. They didn't pay him $25 million to watch Frank throw passes to me. I didn't know how the hell they expected us to build any kind of chemistry when Neil and I hadn't been in one huddle together and the season started in a week. Neil and I were cool, but when you're in the huddle, relationships take on a whole new meaning. That's when **character** and **chemistry** are built. That's what you take to the other team when it's just you and them battling on the field. Frank needed the work. Hell, this made no sense to me. But a lot of things with this team were starting to make no sense.

I played in the game, yeah, but hardly most of it. They

called me in mainly on third down situations, but Reich—even though he was getting the work—wasn't finding me despite the fact that I was open all day. ***"You want Neil's job, you better start finding the open man,"*** I yelled at Reich in the huddle.

He looked kind of shocked.

"I'm open for hours out there, you better stop looking at everyone else. You need to see me. Just get me the ball, I'll take care of the rest."

We lost. I ended up with three catches for 53 yards. Hardly what I should have had.

But I did score a touchdown—my first in the NFL—even though it was just a preseason game and didn't really count. Don't try telling my family that. Or me, either.

It was third-and-21 from the 21-yard line. Fred Baxter had actually caught a touchdown pass the previous play, but it was called back when they flagged us for delay of game.

And then it was my turn. I broke up and then left and did a sweet little post move on Larry Brown in the end zone. The catch was mine. **My family was jumping and screaming** in the end zone. I felt pretty great, scoring on Brown and on the team I'd had so much history with. Even if it was the preseason. Even if there was a bounty on my black ass. The hunter never got close.

BRONCOS **31** ....Jets 6
COLTS **21** ....Jets 7

The Denver game was a disaster. The Indianapolis game was a joke. And before I knew it we were 0–2, I was getting ripped across the country for showing a little life on the field, and Joe Theismann, a washed-up old quarterback who *thinks he's* **God's gift** to football, was *calling* **me** *a jerk.* What was that all about?

I knew we'd lose to Denver. The week of practice leading up to the game told me the team was in trouble. I'd already found out that Rich Kotite *CAN'T COACH* and Ron Erhardt didn't know *WHAT THE HELL* he was doing with the offense. He and I were still going at it. Pat Kirwan kept telling me that I needed to listen to the man because he'd been to the Super Bowl. Well, Dan Reeves has been to three Super Bowls and he can't coach worth shit. How far are you going to get when your entire offensive scheme is run, run, throw on third down for five yards, then punt?

Kotite and Erhardt have been around, true. But what worked **40 years ago** just ain't cutting it now. These coaches were so confused. And they were all afraid. I think they'd just been in the tank so long they didn't know how to win. There was no enthusiasm whatsoever. I passed Kotite in the hall and he just walked by without saying anything. I said, "What's up?" but he just kept on walking. He was already feeling the heat and this was only the first week of the season.

For Denver, our two big linemen, Jumbo Elliott and David Williams, were out. I knew that was going to kill us on the line, but I never thought we'd give up **nine sacks**—eight on O'Donnell, who was growing older by the minute out there. I swear I saw more gray on his head in the fourth quarter.

Denver's got a solid team, and they were mixing things up on defense on us. We never adjusted. Of course, I had no chance to adjust because I hardly played. I caught a pass in the first quarter but O'Donnell had stepped across the line of scrimmage so it didn't count. Believe it or not, that was the **last pass** that came my way until the game was decided. By then O'Donnell was messed up and Frank Reich had come in to take the rest of the beating. He heaved one 50 yards downfield and I was there to pull it in. **One catch for 50 yards.** Oh, well. At least it helped my average.

O'Donnell called the game ugly. Kotite said it was like a flash fire. I called it depressing. We had 174 yards total offense. The only bright spot was our running back Adrian Murrell, who rushed 17 times for 94 yards. I guess he got through the line because all the defensive guys were busy busting up on Neil.

Our huddles were lifeless. We were getting killed, but it was like nobody really cared. When Webster Slaughter scored, he was met with a bunch of empty high-fives. The most energy I saw all day came when Denver's big outside linebacker, Bill Romanowski, got right up in my face.

"Get the fuck out of my way, rookie," he said, pushing me aside.

I didn't move.

"You old," I said. "Get out of the game. You old, man."

He just glared at me. But at least someone was doing something, *trying to stir things up.*

Most of my family had flown out to Denver for the game. Some friends of mine from Denver had a little dinner party for everyone at the hotel the night before. I know they're my people, but most of them were hard-core Broncos fans. What was telling was that not once did someone try to give me shit over how we were going to get our butts kicked. They knew. I knew. The Jets have the reputation as losers and even with all these new big-money changes, my team was flatlining already. *We had no emotion, no energy, no* **hunger.** Not even enough to stir up a rivalry with the Denver fans, much less the Denver team.

As we flew home that night after the game I was down, but not disheartened. Things had to get better. Something was going to have to change. I was going to have to step up.

"Time to start acting like a football team," I announced as I walked into the locker room the morning after the Denver game. Guys looked up, startled.

"I can deal with playing on a sorry team, but not on a team with no heart," I said. **"Time to stop acting scared."**

I meant it, too. I didn't know why all these guys were acting so afraid to be themselves. Nobody was going to win anything with guys scared to put some fire under their play. When I scored against Oakland, I had exactly two guys come up and congratulate me. And neither of them was Kotite or Erhardt. After the game reporters asked me how I felt scoring my first TD.

"Been there, done that," I said to them, but I didn't mean it. I was embarrassed that we hadn't celebrated at all after that. It was like nobody cared, even though that was the first touchdown we'd scored in the entire preseason. There was no celebration. Where were the 15 guys on the field jumping on each other, getting a penalty? With me on the team, we were going to do that, and if the organization didn't like it, they shouldn't have picked me. **My style is having fun and I ain't gonna change** just because I'm getting paid. They had to adjust to me, because from here on, we were going to play like we cared.

I started talking the noise to guys in the locker room and to other guys in the hallways between meetings. People were listening. Even the veterans. Players started calling me at home. Webster Slaughter came by. Jeff Graham came by. Mo Lewis and Marvin Jones started to pick things up at practice, and people started to feed off them. Things got **lively.** And then things got ***hot.***

On Wednesday after practice, the reporters gathered around me, waiting for me to bring it. So I did.

"Keyshawn, are you happy with the role you're being asked to play?" somebody asked.

"Hell, no," I said, knowing full well I was creating the next day's headlines. But I wasn't going to just stand by and not fight for what I believed in, and we weren't just going to collect paychecks every week. "I should be starting. I should be playing every down. There

is no way I should be sitting on the bench behind anybody on this team. *If I'm not starting, there
is something seriously wrong.* It's
not because of physical ability. It's not because I don't
know the plays. Something is wrong somewhere else if
I'm not starting and not in on every play."

Suddenly, it was on. Papers went wild with that, saying
I was campaigning for my spot, trying to edge ol' boy
Chrebet out of the way. What was I supposed to say, "No,
I like coming in on third downs, getting one pass a game?"

I wanted to start. I truly believed I should be starting
and I wasn't afraid to let anybody know it. If you don't believe in yourself, then you shouldn't be out there on the
field. This wasn't any kind of personal attack on Chrebet.
Yeah, we'd had some words, but as time had gone on,
things had cleared up. He was standing right next to me
when I was talking. The next day the coaches came up to
me and said I shouldn't be discussing my business in the
newspapers.

"Hey," I said. "They asked. I answered."

People got the point. I was **serious.** Practice
started picking up. Players were getting lively. But **all
the energy in the world was not
going to help** our game plan. Neither O'Donnell
nor Reich were throwing me the ball. I'd run a clear
route, be wide open downfield or across the middle, and
they'd dump off to one of the backs or Chrebet for five
and six yards a pop. People noticed. Guys on the sidelines,
mainly Lewis and Jones, started hollering: "Way to go, decoy," and, "Way to clear things out for the other guys."
They were doing it so that Kotite and Erhardt could hear.

Decoy. That was funny. Later they'd say it to the media, **calling me the $15 million decoy.** I had to laugh when I read it the next day. For the most part, even the reporters were cool, writing stories saying, "Let's face it, he makes plays every time he's on the field." Mike Ditka came on TV and said that if he was coaching me, he'd throw to me on every down. Might be a job opening around here real soon. Mike needs to apply.

By Thursday, guys were starting to **rally around me and the energy I'd created** on the field and on the news. Even Erhardt got cool. I was running most of the plays and he was talking to me like I was a person rather than some cardboard cutout. "Key, come run this," he'd say, or, "Key, nice route, way to go." Our pace got stepped up about 80%. By game time, I knew the fans would be seeing an entirely different team out there. We had turned up the heat. If we lost to the Colts, at least we'd go down swinging.

Thursday night was receivers night out. Graham and Web called and we got everyone together—even the guys on the practice squad—and headed into New York City for dinner. Chrebet didn't come with us, but it wasn't a big deal. I had let him know I respected what he'd done for the team and even the attitude he carried with him. And he had let me know that he was fine with me stepping in and taking over. On Friday, they made it official. Coach Mann told me I wouldn't be starting against Indy but that I'd come in for the second series and then start the following week, probably for the rest of my career. *They told Chrebet it was over.* He looked pretty sad, but the bottom line was I knew he wanted to win as much as I did.

He would still play. Hell, we were running four- and five-receiver sets, he was going to have to play. Didn't mean he was going to get the ball. Didn't mean *I* was going to get the ball. O'Donnell still wasn't looking for me.

The night before the Indianapolis game, a couple of us went out to dinner with Lamont Warren, a backup running back for the Colts. Lamont and I had played high-school ball together, winning a city championship at Dorsey High. We had stayed tight. When we walked out of the hotel some kids stopped us for autographs. One of them, not realizing who Lamont was, said to me: "Hey, Keyshawn, ***why don't you go kidnap Marshall Faulk.***" We started laughing. Lamont said, "Hey, I'm for that." I thought, Maybe we should kidnap Neil O'Donnell, too.

By kickoff, the crowd was roaring. It was *COOL running onto the field* for the first home game of the season. Even with last week's mess, the fans were pumped. So were we. I could tell right off that we were going to act like a powerful football team, even if we didn't play like one.

When I finally got the word to get into the game, it was the second series, as Mann had predicted. I ran in with my hand up—some people thought I was being cocky—but I was carrying the play, and the signal was five fingers up. Nothing more. Still, people got on me, but the crowd loved it. They cheered like hell.

However, it wasn't like my presence inspired a lot immediately. We went three and out. On the next drive, on third down and 18 yards to go from our own 41-yard line, O'Donnell got pressured and threw a little shovel pass intended for Richie Anderson. He couldn't get to it and even if he had, we'd still have been punting on the next down. We started the second quarter three and out, too, although I caught one pass on second down for six yards.

Nothing we were running had an **ounce of creativity** to it. It was so bad that at one point in the game, a guy on the Colts came up to me and said, "Hey, dog, you know we know exactly where y'all are going. You so predictable, we know what play you're running before you even do."

We ended up losing the game 21–7. Indianapolis quarterback Jim Harbaugh and their tight end, Ken Dilger, killed us. Dilger finished with seven catches for 156 yards. We had a chance, though: Kyle Brady fumbled on the two-yard line. But we were hit with 15 penalties for 100 yards. You can't beat a *high school* team if you have 15 penalties. And Hugh Douglas did something I'd never seen in any game—he roughed the kicker twice.

All day long, all of us receivers were *wide, wide open.* But for some *UNEXPLAINED reason,* O'Donnell couldn't find us. Forget about me—what about Jeff Graham, a million-dollar-a-year man and he finishes with two catches for five yards? O'Donnell only saw Chrebet, or guys open for the short, little, safe passes. Chrebet had a good game—I'm not knocking him. The little kid turned one play big for 44 yards, which really sparked us in the first half. But O'Donnell was afraid to look for anyone beyond five or six yards. Granted, he didn't have a lot of time back there—he was still getting killed on sacks. But we weren't going to beat anybody by playing safe. That was very evident.

At one point in the huddle, I yelled at O'Donnell.

"Quit running the semi-go shit," I said, talking about the stuff where we run half-speed for a short distance, then turn it on to run long. "It's not working. **Let us go full out.** We've been open all day."

He just looked at me with a sort of blank stare. I really don't think he hears us. We were telling him stuff all the time, about what was working, what was not. At some point the quarterback has got to stand up to the coach and tell him what we should be doing. So far, O'Donnell had been nothing but a **STIFF PUPPET** back there.

And Erhardt, man, he was tripping at times. In the third quarter we were sitting third down with two yards to go. He called a play where I go in motion and am supposed to block the cornerback on the opposite side. But the guy I was supposed to cover was too far off, he never dropped down. I saw the outside linebacker coming in, so I switched off and took him out. Adrian Murell ran through the hole for nine yards, first down. When we came off the field, Erhardt was **screaming mad.**

"You blocked the wrong guy," he yelled. "If you'd have stayed with the plan, taken the corner, the play would have developed."

"Hey," I yelled back. "I don't take the linebacker, the play would have developed into minus 10 in the back-field."

Another bright idea came from Erhardt, who decided we'd run a new play—one we hadn't even practiced once—in the fourth quarter. I ran the wrong route, but I got open. The next Monday morning in films he drew a red circle around me.

"Look, this guy didn't even know what he was doing," he told the team. *"Hey, if you're going to talk the talk, you'd better* walk the walk."

"Oh, shut up," somebody yelled from the back.

I was about to speak up when Coach Mann grabbed me by the arm and said, "Key, don't. Don't worry about it."

I didn't. Nor was I worrying about what would become the controversy of the week: my touchdown and my touchdown celebration. Never have I seen people get so worked up over some guys having fun on the field. And most of the critics had no idea what had happened on that field during that drive and what effect celebrating in the end zone had on my team. It was a drive that I thought just might change our season. It certainly changed our attitude. All week long I'd been talking stuff to the media and trying to pump up my teammates. Get them ready to play *football as the game of football SHOULD be played.* And for a few moments there against Indy, it was happening.

It was our last drive before halftime. We started on our own 44-yard line and made it to the Indianapolis 17-yard line after I caught a 14-yarder from O'Donnell. Both Chrebet and Richie Anderson had made big plays, gaining extra yardage because of a couple of **monster blocks** I threw. Nobody knew, until then, that I could block like that. I learned by watching Tony Boselli at USC. He taught me how to hit and hit hard. I almost took the head off David Tate, No. 49 for the Colts, coming right up under his helmet.

"Hey, rookie," he yelled at me. "I play fair, you play fair."

"I play football, just chill, buddy."

"Rookie, do that again and we'll be fighting," said Tate.

"Fine, I'll beat your ass all the way to the bus," I said. "Bring it on."

Our huddle overheard the exhange.

"Don't take no shit off him, Key," someone said.

We were starting to feel like things were going right. On second-and-10 from the 17, O'Donnell threw to Chrebet, who cut inside to gain 11 yards and a first down. First-and-goal. I sprinted over to Chrebet and lifted him up.

"That's it baby, that's it," I screamed at him. And then we ran back to the huddle, **PUMPED,** slapping guys on their helmets.

"That's the way, that's the way. C'mon, now, keep it up. Let's get in there," I was saying. "We gotta do it now."

Guys started to feel it. I could feel it. Right then, for those moments, we had an attitude. An attitude of some-one who wasn't backing down for **nothing** *and* **nobody.**

After it was all over some of the guys who had been with the team for a few years told me they hadn't felt that kind of charge in a long, long time.

O'Donnell overthrew Murrell on first down and then on second-and-goal, Harry Boatswain jumped offsides so we were pushed back to the 11-yard line.

"No problem," I said. "Do it on this one. Neil, you gotta find me."

But he didn't even look. On second down, O'Donnell threw at Jeff Graham, but the Colts DB, Dedric Mathis, stepped in and broke up the play. I refused to give in. We had less than a minute to play in the half, and one more chance at the end zone. We huddled up and I screamed at O'Donnell.

"Just find me, put it close," I said. "I'll catch it. I'll get us six."

Finally, on third down, he dropped back, looking to the right, then to the middle, and then after what seemed like forever, looked left to where I was wide open in the end zone. I had been open for so long that I almost got covered again. It was a bad pass, low, at my knees. But I leaned down and scooped it in. We had scored. I had scored. Something had worked.

After that, it was **madness.**

Nothing was planned. Nothing was set. I hadn't even thought about what I'd do if I got into the end zone. Before the game Erhardt had told us that weak old Paul Brown cliché: "If you get in the end zone, act like you've been there before."

Well, screw that. I hadn't been there before. And the Jets hadn't been there since last season. We were riding on emotion that drive. We were proving something, not to the rest of the league or even to the Colts, but to ourselves: that we were capable of putting something together. We had 31 seconds left to play in the half and were down just 14–7. Maybe I could spark a turnover on the kickoff, do something to pull us even by the break. I tore off my helmet and **spiked** the ball. Harry Boatswain and about 20 other guys came rushing into the end zone, where they knocked me to the turf.

"Yeah! Yeah!" everyone was screaming.

They felt it, too. When I fell, I tore the skin off my left palm on the turf and scraped both of my knees and an elbow. But I didn't care. I loved it. That's what playing football is all about.

I've celebrated touchdowns before. A lot of people know about my junior college days, when after one TD catch I ran into the stands and grabbed a coke, and after another I ran out of the stadium onto a hill to see the sunset. I even celebrated when I was at USC, getting a 15-yard penalty for taunting when we played Cal. The Jets certainly knew those stories. They knew what I cared most about was getting this team fired up and winning games. Kotite told the media he liked my swagger.

"Keyshawn is a football player first and foremost, and he's a team player," he said. "I like the **ENERGY** he brings. He thinks he can make this team better and **you gotta LOVE that.**"

Not everyone did. I was ripped around the league by people who had nothing better to do than make waves with their mouths. Theismann was one of them.

"Disgusting," he had said on ESPN's *Prime Monday* when asked about the TD celebration. *"He's a jerk. He acted like a jerk, he sounds like a jerk, he's playing like a jerk."*

This from a guy who had never met me, never said one word to me. He knew nothing about me.

"Who's the real jerk?" I asked the media when they asked for my response. "For a grown man to say that about another grown man, it's disrespectful. It makes no sense."

The next week on ESPN's *NFL Countdown* show,

Theismann apologized. All of that mess, all the hype, all the attention he drew to himself and his little TV gig—in the end, he just looked **stupid.**

So did other people. Mostly TV and radio guys who just like to flap their mouths and stir up shit. Mike Francesa was blasting me on WFAN, but his partner, Chris Russo, the Mad Dog, was defending me. Francesa was on me about smiling on the sidelines as the game came to a close and we had taken another beating.

"What am I supposed to do, cry?" I asked.

Media's crazy.

The fans, though, *the fans were cool.* I listened in to the callers on WFAN. One guy called in and told Francesa he was crazy for ripping me.

"That celebration was the most exciting thing we've seen in that stadium in 20 years," he said.

The only problem was that we were 0–2 and all the emotion and energy in the world wasn't going to change that. I'd never been 0–2 before, ever, in my entire football career. And I wasn't liking it at all.

DOLPHINS 36 .... Jets 27
GIANTS 13 .... Jets 6

I've lost before. I've lost some big, big games, in fact.

We lost in the semifinals of the high school city championships my senior year at Dorsey. We lost when I was at West Los Angeles (junior) College, and we lost when I played for USC. **I hate losing.** I've never equated football with losing. Never. I hate losing even more than I hate Notre Dame, and the only reason I hate Notre Dame is because when I was playing in college, we lost to them—twice.

But back then it didn't seem as frustrating as it does now. In every one of those games we were in them all the way. We didn't give up. We didn't give anything away. We went down, yeah, but we went down kicking and swinging.

So maybe it's a pro thing. Cash that paycheck on Monday and all your cares and woes with it. *I know it's a Jets thing.* I think the Cowboys and the 49ers hate losing as much as I do.

Damn, we had a 14-point lead on the Dolphins at Miami and **choked.** I thought we'd win the game. A few other guys did, too. Adrian Murrell was running his butt off, eating right through the line. He thought we could win. The receiving corps thought we could, too. We figured Adrian would get our game out on the ground and then we would pounce. That's the way it was designed to work. But we should have known better—winning just wasn't part of the game plan.

"They've got a bunch of no-name young guys down there," Erhardt said the Monday before the game as we watched film. "They're 2–0 and aren't looking to get beat. They're tough, I tell you, a tough group. Don't underestimate them because they're young and you don't know who they are."

"Man," I told Jeff Graham later, "they're talking like the Dolphins have already won the game."

The ATTITUDE was all wrong. That's definitely a Jets thing. So it was a huge surprise to me that we jumped out in front 14–0. Aaron Glenn took an interception 100 yards on one of the sweetest runs I'd seen in a long while. Dan Marino was throwing for the end zone, and Glenn just stepped in and took it all the way. Then Webster Slaughter caught a 30-yard pass from O'Donnell for another. Well, actually Neil threw the ball about six yards and Web did the rest.

Unfortunately, our lead lasted about as long as **_Neil's SCRAGGLY-ASS beard._** Marino hit Stanley Pritchett for 74 yards and a touchdown on the first play of their next drive. Then they pulled even on their next possession with a strong drive and a four-yard run by a guy I'd seen do that a hundred times—my old roommate Karim Abdul Jabbar.

Karim was Sharmon Shah when we played high school ball at Dorsey, but we all called him "Wood" because his real nickname was "Hollywood." Not because of his personality—he's about the most laid-back guy I know—but because **we knew he was going to be *A STAR*** in the league. He had ability from day one at Dorsey as our starting running back. Lamont Warren was a running back, too, but our quarterback got hurt and Lamont had to switch. Wood stepped right in and never stopped. We knew Wood would make it. He took care of business not only on the field but also in school, and ended up at UCLA. Lamont did, too, and ended up at Colorado. I didn't, doing poorly on the SATs twice; but I thought I'd be able to talk my way into a four-year college.

I had been recruited like crazy by all the top schools around the country. They saw my first semester grades my senior year, which weren't all that hot, but I convinced them that I'd pull them up second semester and pass the SATs. I thought that if they wanted me badly enough, they'd get me into school. *I tried every trick in the book* to get into college without actually having to go through the system. **It's how I had gotten by all my life.** I called coaches, asking them to hook me up, worked all these connections, trying to befriend people who could do something for me. Don Pellum, now the coach at Oregon, was doing everything he could to get me into Cal, calling his buddies, everything. But when it came down to it, I couldn't get in.

Once the four-year coaches realized I wasn't going to make it, they tried a different approach. They still called, but now they were talking about stashing me in a junior college nobody had ever heard of. Then I had the jucos calling, too. And some of my high school coaches who had gone on to community colleges were calling. It got pretty nuts.

There were a few of my crew from Dorsey who didn't pass the SATs, either. Marlin Lewis, Derek Hazely, Skeats. **We were pretty embarrassed** that we had talked all this shit and then had no place to go. We felt it would be humiliating to go to a junior college in Los Angeles because it looked like, "Dang, you didn't go to a four-year with all that talent." *So we decided to go to a juco as* FAR AWAY *as possible.*

Cal wanted me to go to a juco up in northern California. Miami wanted me to go to Northeast Oklahoma Junior College. A couple of schools in Texas wanted me to go to jucos in Texas. And Barney Farrar, now an assistant coach at Rice University, had been recruiting me hard for Clemson and wanted me to go to Tri-County Tech in Anderson, South Carolina. I had always liked Clemson and Farrar was COOL, so Skeats and I said, OKAY.

They couldn't believe their luck. And they were even more stunned that we paid for everything ourselves and never asked for a dime. I still had a sizable stash from my ticket-scalping days, and was able to buy plane tickets and hook us up with an apartment. Our plan was to go to school at Tri-County Tech and then be eligible to transfer after one year. Every morning we'd be in class, then get a ride from sombody and watch Clemson's practice. It was hard on both Skeats and me. We were high school heroes in Los Angeles, which might as well have been halfway across the world from where we were now. **The South.** *What a trip.*

Nobody on the Clemson team had the slightest idea of what kind of player I was, except, of course, for the coaches. None of the players could believe I came all the way from L.A. to sit on their bleachers and watch practice. Skeats lasted two weeks until he got into trouble with some married woman whose husband was threatening to kill him. He got his butt back to L.A., and fast. I stayed for another week and decided I was too far from home, and so I headed back to L.A., too, with no idea of what I would do.

Eventually I settled on West Los Angeles College because one of their assistant coaches, Darryl Holmes, had been our offensive coordinator and line coach at Dorsey. Holmes always gave it to me straight and I figured it was the right choice. And so I moved in with Skeats and his mom, Everett, who used to feed me a lot when I was in high school. They really didn't have the room, **but they had a roof** and that was all that mattered right then.

I got this wonderful, brilliant idea that I was going to load up on classes at West L.A., finish school in one year, and then get into a Division I university. I didn't play football that fall—actually, I did until the coach, Rob Hager, kicked me off the team for not having the "proper attitude." Shit, I didn't want to play some sorry ball for some sorry juco. At least that's what I was thinking then. **I was still trying to scam my way through life,** and for a while, it was working.

By spring I had a bunch of credits and all the coaches who were calling me were saying, "Damn, he's close, he's so close. We can sign him, he's close to making it." I had all these guys believing that I was going to pass all my classes, get enough credits to enroll in school in August, and be eligible that fall. I even took recruiting trips to Cal, Mississippi State, and Texas Tech—that's how much

I had convinced them I was going to be able to transfer.

And I actually signed with Mississippi State. But then the **big, bad NCAA** came crashing down. The rule book caught me. Nobody—not one of those big administrators—had bothered to look at the fine print, which said you had to spend two years in a junior college, that you couldn't do it in one.

So I stayed at West L.A., eventually moving closer to school, into a small one-bedroom apartment with six other guys. Nobody had any money, so to reduce the rent, **we let in anyone** who wanted to move in. Not surprisingly, we eventually got thrown out of there for having too many people in the apartment and causing too many problems. The manager simply stopped accepting our rent.

From there, I moved to West Covina, where Skeats was going to Mt. San Antonio Community College for a bit. Eight of us were living in a two-bedroom apartment and that got to be too much, too. Finally, I moved in with a friend named Dave Darnell and his mom in Inglewood. The neighborhood was terrible, and she had just gotten caught up in the mess. Like so many people in the inner city, the **trouble inched toward her house daily** and eventually her home was surrounded by gangs and drugs and violence. It's tough on anybody, but especially on a mom. I knew.

Living there, well, I was grateful for a bed. But living there also changed my life, for the second time. The first had come earlier after I spent a stretch in a juvenile detention camp for scalping stolen football tickets. More on that later. This change was a lot more serious.

It happened one night late in April 1993, before my

last season at West L.A. I was rolling in about 11 p.m. after going to the movies. The guys I was with dropped me off at the curb outside Mrs. Darnell's house and, out of habit, I checked the streets before getting out. The neighborhood was in the middle of gang warfare at the time and you had to check out the scene before you did anything, even if you weren't into any of it. As I closed the car door, I saw a car with dark, tinted windows pulling around the corner, real slow. Right then I knew something suspicious was going on. So I broke into a light jog up the driveway and as I was going, I looked back, and the door of that car opened up and somebody started hanging out. I took off running and the guy just started shooting. ***Pop, pop, pop, aiming right at me.*** It was like something out of the movies, and something I'd seen dozens of times in my neighborhood growing up. But I didn't have any problems with anybody—in any gang. Hell, I was in college. I was an athlete. I was straight. Nobody was going to mess with me.

But this was a Bloods-infested neighborhood. It could have been Crips thinking they were shooting at Bloods, Bloods thinking they were shooting at Bloods; could have been someone looking to rob somebody who panicked. To this day I still don't know why they were shooting and why at me. I ran inside the house, thankful I was **still breathing.**

Dave's mom was on the floor, having heard the shots. She looked up at me and screamed.

"Keyshawn! Your leg!"

I looked down to see **a stream of blood** coming through my socks and pant leg. ***I'd been shot*** *for the first time in my life* and it scared the hell out of me. This was my leg, my future. If my leg was messed up, so was everything I'd finally gotten on track for. The next day I was supposed to work out at West L.A. for the college scouts. I was going to go to bed early. Instead, I was rushing to the hospital and spending most of the night on a bed in the emergency room, not knowing if I'd make the workout or ever play football again. After all I'd been through, I was on track to graduate with an Associate of Arts degree. But here I was, laid up, shot.

"Son, you're very lucky," the doctor told me. He was holding a **metal 9mm bullet** that he had taken from my leg. "Had this bullet hit two inches differently, the bone would have been shattered."

"How's my leg?" I asked. "Can I run?"

"Anybody with weak muscles, I'd be saying not for a while," he said. "If your legs weren't so strong, if you hadn't had on those thick socks, you'd be in trouble. As it is now, **you'll be fine.**"

I was tough, and as strong as leather. In anticipation of the workout, I'd been working hard in the weight room and on the track. I always thought it was to make me better, not to prevent me from a serious injury. **It shook me up, bad.**

But two days after the shooting, I was running again, and the scouts came back out the next week. My coaches explained the situation and made it very clear that it wasn't me doing the bad stuff, it was bad stuff finding me.

And that's when, boom, I knew I had to move. Trouble can find you anywhere, but when you're young and black and living in South Central, you're a big target for any fool who decides to come along firing a gun, proving himself. Nobody outside of my own area knew who I was. I had never shot anybody, never done anything to anybody in a gang who'd want to harm me. ***I was just a warm body waiting to get blown away.*** I couldn't let that happen.

So Dave and I borrowed money from a bunch of people and found ourselves a two-bedroom apartment in Culver City, just a few blocks from school. We borrowed some furniture from friends and took the rest from discarded piles in alleys. Where we were staying wasn't exactly clean, but it was relatively safe, and for the first time in my life I had a bedroom to myself. I was 20 years old.

Dave couldn't cut the rent, though. He ran out of money fast and I found myself strapped. I borrowed money from Tim Shannon, a friend I used to hang out with when he was playing at USC and I was a ball boy.

Man, my ball boy days were wild. I got involved with a couple of other players and ball boys in a **bike-stealing scam** on campus. I was just a little kid, so I'd go steal a bike and then take it to a player's room, where we'd strip it and re-paint it and sell it back, sometimes to the dude we'd stolen it from.

One day this player's roommate came home and caught us stripping down a bike.

"You can't have people here doing stuff like that," he said, real serious.

"It's from the frat house," our buddy said.

The roommate thought for a minute.

"Oh, well, if you can't beat 'em, join 'em."

Other times, some of the neighborhood kids and some

of the ball boys and I would wait until the ROTC guys went out to march, then sneak in their classroom and rifle through their backpacks and steal their money. We were **bad.** But we were **hungry,** not that that makes it right.

Guys on the team took care of us. Marcus Allen and Ronnie Lott were always giving us food and stuff. And Tim Shannon took care of me for so many years that it was natural for me to hit him up for $200 when Dave moved. I had no idea it would come back to haunt me when I was at USC. Tim had become an agent and the NCAA tried to say he gave me money as an agent.

Even with the $200, I still needed someone to pay half the rent if I was going to stay there. So I called Wood, who was still living with his parents near Dorsey. And that's how we became roommates. *We got along like brothers.* All through summer and my last season playing, all we talked about was football and how we were going to make it to the league. We had a lot of dreams back then, although he was a lot closer to his than I was. Maybe he realized it, I don't know, but it hurt me that he was a step ahead of me. He was in a D-1 school and making it. I was stuck in junior college, a lifetime away, it seemed, from being where I wanted to be. My fault, I realized then. I hadn't done what he had done.

But getting shot and seeing Wood working out every day helped get me back into the right process. He really was an inspiration to me. I'd watch him run for 500 yards on TV and know that I should be there, too. I wasn't about to do anything to jeopardize my opportunity. Even with school. *I had tried the scam route, and it didn't work.* I was working hard, trying to stay in class and do the stuff it took to get into a Division I school.

Wood also brought with him a lot of stability, something I really had never had. He had a dad and a stepmother, both strong, caring people who claimed our whole crew as their sons. They'd come by and talk to us like people, not like kids, and make sure we had our heads on right. And they brought food, which was a big, big deal to me and the West L.A. guys who hung out almost all the time at the apartment.

Before Wood moved in, the only thing we'd eat for days was this special potato and onion dish we used to make. That and maybe a can of corn. Sometimes some guys and I would go to the store and steal meat because we hadn't had it in so long and we were so hungry after practice. Some of the coaches knew what we were doing, but could only warn us not to get caught. Sometimes they'd slip us a few dollars, but they weren't making much either. **It was hard to practice with no food in our stomachs,** so we did what we could.

It was shortly after that year that Wood decided to reaffirm his faith and embrace the Muslim religion. We all thought it was pretty cool, but we had to laugh when we heard what Muslim name he had been given—Karim Abdul Jabbar. *I guess the brother who named Wood didn't follow hoops.* Even the jersey number was the same. Reporters went crazy on that. Still do. Especially when the Dolphins spelled his name wrong on his jersey. He didn't think it was funny. But that didn't last long. Heck, Karim's got nothing to worry about. The Dolphins are winning and Karim is tearing up the field.

Especially against us. He finished the game with 124 yards on 23 carries and two touchdowns, and the Dolphins won 36–27. I would love to have given Karim those yards, hell, have given him double, but have beaten his ass on the scoreboard.

As for me, well, **the good news was that I started**—finally. And I caught another touchdown pass, reaching up high and pulling it down with about three guys around me. I didn't even have to jump. The bad news was that the game was the same-ol', same-ol'. I caught *six passes for 59 YARDS and a TOUCH-DOWN,* but basically it was a repeat of all of our practices and the first two games of the season: O'Donnell couldn't get me the ball and Erhardt was stuck in some funk from the forties.

Take our last drive in the first half. With 52 seconds left, O'Donnell found me for six yards and a first down. The next play, with just thirty seconds on the clock, he threw up the middle to Richie Anderson for seven yards.

Up the middle?

"Why are you only looking to one side out there, to the easy, short pass?" I hollered as I ran back into the huddle. **O'Donnell didn't even look at me.**
He threw two more incomplete passes, and after two penalties we had first-and-15 from the Miami 48 with 16 seconds left in the half. And what does the $25 million man do? Throws short to Anderson. Thankfully it was in-

complete. Next play, with 11 seconds on the clock, O'Donnell keeps the ball and runs to midfield.

Midfield?

Before the game, I'd seen Miami's new coach, Jimmy
Johnson, on the field with his girlfriend. Jimmy's a guy
I'd love to be playing for. He's got discipline—which we
have none of—and he's got heart. Bottom line, he's not
going to lose.

"Jimmy, save me," I said, walking over to him. "Save
my career. Trade all your picks. Get me to Miami."

We both were laughing.

"I'd sure like to," he said. "But I just don't think we can
get that done right now. But if *I had you, I'd be throwing to you a **hell** of a lot more.*"

I talked to Karim on the field after the game. I'm happy
for him. He's one of the best guys I know. He was the Dolphins' third pick and they got a steal. I'm making a lot
more money, but he's got a lot more than I do right now—
he's playing on a winning team and he's getting the ball.

"Wood," I said to him after the game. "You tore us
up, baby."

"Your time's coming," he assured me.

I hope he's right.

I really did think we'd be good this year. I talked a lot
about how you have to find chemistry and gel and all
that, but I really thought we'd take the league by storm. I
thought we were going to the Super Bowl, or at least to
the playoffs. Before the season started, I thought we'd win
the first few games, but that I'd be a little rusty because

of my holdout. I knew that by the third or fourth game of the season, we'd be flying.

I don't know when I've ever miscalculated so badly.

Especially against the Giants.

All week long the press had built this game into something of a farce.

"We'll have all the highlights from the NFL . . . and from the Jets–Giants game," the clowns on Fox said in their preview.

"The Peyton Manning bowl," *someone else was calling it.*

Both teams were 0–3 with not a lot of hope on the horizon. And even though we had beaten them in preseason and I really thought we could beat them again, we stunk and we lost.

I'd have **run decoy all day to have won that game,** and never said a word. It wasn't the rivalry—I didn't know anything about the history of the teams, the fights, the animosity between the two owners—I just didn't want to be 0–4.

By game time the rain was falling pretty steadily. Not as bad as during the Indianapolis game, when we made history by having our game called off for 32 minutes because of lightning, but steady. That was a bad sign in itself because it was going to make it hard on us to run crisp routes. But the worst sign came when **the dude messed up the national anthem.** I should have known then that it was all over.

Basically, it was.

I started but didn't have a pass thrown my way until there was 3:20 left in the second quarter.

Earlier in the half, on a third down and eight situation, O'Donnell threw a three-yard route to Richie Anderson just to get rid of the ball. On third-and-13, he dropped back for a second and then dumped off to Anderson again for a two-yard gain.

We all ran back to the sidelines as Anderson got up, stopped well before the first down, and slammed the ball down.

"Why the hell are you throwing to me?" Anderson yelled.

O'Donnell didn't look at him, either. *Guess it's* **NOT** *just me.*

At halftime, just before we headed out for the start of the third quarter, Kotite pulled me aside.

"We need you to do something, fire up this team, make a big play," he said.

"Hey, how can I do that when I'm not getting the ball?" I answered.

"You'll get it, you'll get it," he assured me. **"Just make something happen."**

They tried. O'Donnell overthrew me three times when I was open on sideline patterns. I caught a fourth attempt for 14 yards. And that was it. I can't make something happen if the ball isn't in my hands. I can block, but that isn't going to get us from being behind to being ahead. We lost 13–6. It was about as bad as I've felt in years. As the clock wound down, I walked over to the end of the bench, frustrated to the point of tears. How the hell were we going to fix this?

Our high-priced quarterback now ranked 27th in the

league in completion percentage (56.7%) and 18th in yardage-per-completion—less than six yards. That—and the play-calling by Erhardt—told the entire story of why we were 0–4. Our defense had done a heck of a job, but **O'Donnell was still SCARED and Erhardt was still OLD.**

Neil blamed the rain. Kotite blamed Erhardt. Erhardt blamed Neil.

David Letterman even made fun of the entire farce the next night.

"I heard JFK Jr. and his new bride are trying to find a nice, quiet, private place to spend their honeymoon," he said in his opening monologue. "Well, what about the end zones at Giants Stadium?"

I sure hadn't spent much time there.

After the game, a bunch of us went to a place called the Shark Bar in Manhattan. It's a cool restaurant that caters predominantly to an African-American crowd. They play good music, serve good soul food, and, basically, people leave us alone.

We had a big table—myself, Jeff Graham, Victor Green, Aaron Glenn, Marcus Coleman, Jeff Faulkner, Lonnie Young, and our various people.

"Is Kotite in trouble?" someone asked.

"Can't be," I said. "Because anyone they bring in is still going to lose."

"Because of Erhardt," Graham said.

"Exactly," I said. "Because Erhardt is running the show. They both need to be fired right now, but that's not going to happen."

We sat around for a while talking about the game, glad

to be out of the rain. The music was nice and the place was warm. **We started talking about who we'd like to play for.** The obvious names came up: Jimmy Johnson, Barry Switzer, Bill Parcells. And a few less obvious names: Steve Spurrier, Terry Bowden.

One thing we all agreed on: A change needed to be made.

"You know what's scary?" I said. ***"We could go 0−16,*** not win a game all year."

Nobody said a thing.

For the first time all season, Erhardt was calling the right plays. He was mixing things up and our running game was opening up the pass. Just like we practiced. We were balling. Defense. Offense. The whole package. We had been moving the ball all day on the Washington Redskins and were down just 24–16 at the start of the fourth quarter. **I was thinking W.**

And then the officials stepped up and **killed us.**

We had driven from our own 23-yard line to the Washington seven. On second-and-goal, O'Donnell tossed a short pass to tight end Fred Baxter, who caught it, took two steps, and fumbled out of bounds. The refs called it incomplete.

"How can it be incomplete when he takes two steps?" I argued. "Man, I've been getting held all day and they can't see that. Refs are going to job us, I can feel it."

The crowd at RFK Stadium was going crazy. *Damn, that place is loud,* fans yelling "Kotite sucks" and "Jets suck." We couldn't hear a thing when we lined up.

"Throw me the ball, just give me the damn ball," I kept yelling, as usual, at O'Donnell when we huddled up. Usually he ignored me. But this time he turned right to my face.

"I can't change the play they bring in," he yelled back.

"Haven't you ever heard of an audible?" I wanted to

95

scream. "Are you a *robot* or a *quarterback?*"

But I kept quiet. It was no time to start picking a fight with my own quarterback. Not if I wanted the ball, not if I wanted to score. Which I did and I would, if he'd just look my way.

Second down, O'Donnell misses Adrian Murrell. As usual, I was wide open in the end zone. Fortunately, Stanley Richard was caught hanging all over Alex Van Dyke. Even the referees couldn't ignore that. We got a first down at the three-yard line.

"Key," O'Donnell hollered as he stepped into the huddle, looking right at me. "You wanted it, you got it."

Finally.

We broke the huddle and the crowd stepped it up, the roar as loud as any I'd ever experienced. Even though we couldn't hear a thing and the Skins were trying to stop us from scoring, I was loving every minute of it. This is why I play football, I was thinking. The juice was flowing, the adrenaline pumping. I was getting the ball and everyone in that stadium was trying to stop me. This was our chance to get in a position to win this thing. We score on this drive, convert on a two-point play, the game's dead even and we've got the mo'.

The ball was snapped and I ran a short post route to the end zone. I turned and saw the ball sailing toward me.

"Too high, too high," I thought. "Gotta reach. Gotta stretch."

I leaped into the air, my arms stretched way in front of me, waiting for the ball to drop down. I felt cornerback Tom Carter breathing next to me stride for stride. As I went up, so did he. As I caught the ball, he was right

First pick in the 1996 NFL Draft. Standing alongside NFL commissioner Paul Tagliabue.
(courtesy of Johnson personal collection)

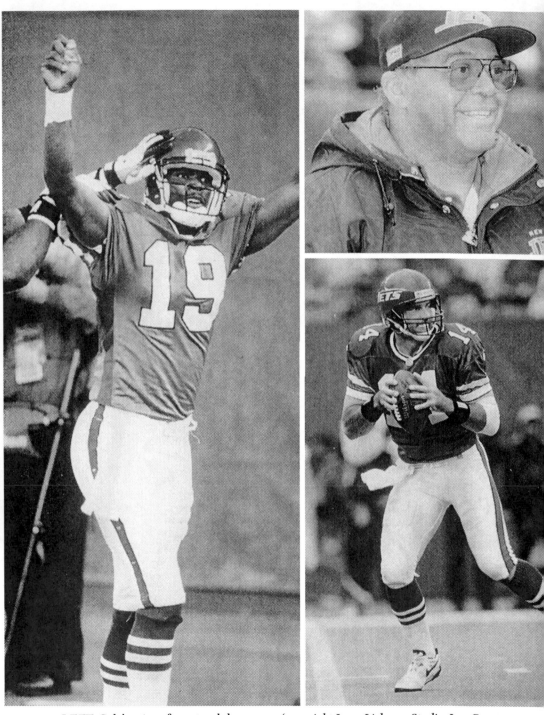

LEFT: Celebrating after a touchdown pass. *(copyright Jerry Liebman Studio, Inc. Courtesy of the New York Jets)* RIGHT, TOP: Receivers coach Rich Mann. *(copyright Jerry Liebman Studio, Inc. Courtesy of the New York Jets)* BOTTOM: Neil O'Donnell drops back to pass against the New York Giants. *(copyright Al Pereira. Courtesy of the New York Jets)*

LEFT: Former New York Jets head coach Rich Kotite. *(copyright Al Pereira. Courtesy of the New York Jets)* RIGHT: Offensive coordinator Ron Erhardt. *(copyright Jerry Liebman Studio, Inc. Courtesy of the New York Jets)*

TOP: Posing with Dolphin rookie running back and childhood friend Karim Abdul Jabbar after a loss to Miami. *(courtesy of Johnson personal collection)*

RIGHT: Never afraid to talk to the media. *(courtesy of Johnson personal collection)*

TOP: Flanked by my college coach, John Robinson (left), and sportscaster Jim Hill. *(courtesy of Johnson personal collection)*

LEFT: An All-American at USC. *(courtesy of Johnson personal collection)*

The Crew: (left to right) Reynaldo "Skeats" Spalding, me, Tamecus Peoples, Marlin Lewis, Derek Hazely, Tony Graham, and Jets wide receiver Jeff Graham. *(courtesy of Johnson personal collection)*

LEFT: My mom, Vivian Jessie, with my daughter, Maia. *(courtesy of Johnson personal collection)* RIGHT: Back in my ball boy days with former USC player Tim Shannon, now a sports agent in Los Angeles. I'm the one holding the Pepsi. *(courtesy of Johnson personal collection)*

TOP: Graduation day with Shikiri and Maia. *(courtesy of Johnson personal collection)*
BOTTOM: Marlin Lewis (right) and me at a Key's Kids event. *(courtesy of Johnson personal collection)*

Hello, New York. *(courtesy of Johnson personal collection)*

there. I pulled it down, squeezed it tight, landed one foot and then the other in the end zone. Suddenly, I felt Carter strip the ball away. No problem, I thought. I broke the plane. I landed my feet. I scored the touchdown.

"Six, baby, six!" I was screaming.

We were celebrating, arms in the air, already thinking about the two-point conversion attempt, when I turned back and saw one official waving the play off and another throwing a flag. The third official lowered his arms from the touchdown position and they moved aside to confer.

"What the hell are you talking about?" I yelled, ripping off my helmet. "It was a touchdown … a touchdown … what the hell are you doing?"

They kept talking. Finally, inexplicably, they ruled pass interference on me—for what?—and an interception.

"Get the replay, get the replay," I screamed, forgetting that they didn't have that anymore. *You're blowing it. You're blowing it."*

Everyone was arguing, the players with one ref, Kotite with another. Kotite's face turned bright red and he was yelling as loudly as I'd ever heard him. O'Donnell was still stuck in a touchdown pose and I was just stomping around the end zone, incredulous that this could happen in a game supposedly officiated by the best refs in football.

"They took it from you," Webster Slaughter said. "Took it right from you."

"Man," Alex Van Dyke said, shaking his head. *"That's a cold call."*

Ironically, a few weeks earlier I had shot a promo commercial for ESPN with Kobe Bryant. In the ad, *Sports-*

Center anchor Stuart Scott was teaching me how to act.

"What do you say, Keyshawn, when the ref makes a bad call?" he asked, in the classroom setting.

"I say, 'That was a bad call, ref.' "

"No," Stuart screamed. "You say, 'That was a bullshit call. That was a bullshit call.' "

Obviously, in the commercial they bleeped out the appropriate words. On the field, faced with the same situation, I didn't. And, I added a few of the m-f words, too.

"Stupid-ass referees," I said later. "I know this is a crooked town with all the politicians and slime-throwing that goes on. ***But I thought football, with FOOT-BALL, it'd be straight.***"

I couldn't believe they robbed us like that. I couldn't believe they took away a valid score that might have won the game for us. Above all, I couldn't believe it had happened to me ... again.

It was almost the same play, the same situation. Turn the calendar back five years and **I'm getting screwed all over again.** I was a senior at Dorsey High School and we were battling one of the teams we hated the most: Banning. It was the semifinals of the city championships and we had been picked to win it all.

High school football in California is a lot like it is in Texas, just fewer rednecks. It's just as competitive, and we've got a lot of talent on the West Coast, especially in the inner city of Los Angeles, where little kids grow up dreaming of the Super Bowl. When I was a kid, I played Pop Warner football and Little League baseball. Kids do the same things now, but for a while there was nothing to do in South Central. There was no Little League, no Boy Scouts, no Boys and Girls Clubs. *The neighborhood parks were taken over by the* drug dealers, and running with a gang became a kid's only option for afterschool activity.

People don't really realize it, but a lot of the problems in the inner city are caused by the lack of opportunities after school. There just isn't enough for kids to do.

I was lucky. I always had a place to play, **even when I was on the corner selling drugs.**

Doing business always came after practice. Football was what I always cared about the most and why I stayed in school. I wanted to play.

The city playoffs are the hottest thing in Los Angeles during the fall. It's all the football powers from the inner city battling some of the suburban schools for one big prize: bragging rights and a trophy. The atmosphere in L.A. starts hopping at playoff time. People from all over get into it, crowding the games, cheering for the school in their area. *The games get downright vicious* and, sometimes, dangerous, when things get hot.

Dorsey has been a city power for as long as I can remember. I should have gone there straight from junior high school, but my mother had moved to the Valley and I enrolled at Canoga Park because it was close to home. I played my sophomore year there, but the team was sorry.

I think we won two games the entire year. Then I transferred to Pacific Palisades High School, close to Santa Monica, but all along I really wanted to go to Dorsey. Everybody I knew was there and they kept yapping about getting me to switch. I hung out there a lot during the spring of my junior year, watching their team practice.

They were good. They had Lamont Warren (now with the Indianapolis Colts), Karim Abdul Jabbar (then Sharmon Shah), and my boys—Marlin Lewis, Skeats, and Tamecus Peoples—on defense. Those guys would go on to play with me in junior college. Skeats ended up at Iowa and Portland State, Tamecus played a couple of years at Sonoma State until his knee blew out, and Marlin went to Eastern Michigan.

During the summer before my senior year, I was playing summer league basketball at Palisades and then driving to Dorsey to play summer league football. Finally, I used the address of my cousin (Chris Miller, who played this year at USC) as my home and made the transfer. *I was convinced we could win it all* and Dorsey's coach, Paul Knox, said he'd make sure I was featured in the offense enough to attract every major college in the country.

Part of that was right. I did attract every major college. The other would have happened too if—like in the Redskins game—we hadn't gotten **robbed by the refs.**

The parallels between the two situations are strange. In the Dorsey–Banning game, we had been battling even all day long. The crowds were intense, and we were so pumped to beat Banning and go on to the city championship finals. We had so much talent and so much drive, *we couldn't lose.* We weren't going to let that happen.

With two minutes to play in the game we had pulled ahead 20–14 and had moved the ball to the Banning 30-yard line. We were threatening to score to put the game away. Lamont was playing quarterback, and he threw a fade to me in the corner of the end zone. I saw the ball, leaped high, came down with it, and fell to the ground. Travis Davis, a cornerback for Banning who went on to play at Notre Dame and now plays for Jacksonville, had his hands on the ball, too, but I clearly had possession. I had control of the ball. I scored the touchdown. We landed side by side, Travis grappling, trying to take the ball away from me. **I said, "Here, take it," shoved it in his stomach,** and got up.

It wasn't until I was almost to the sidelines, thinking we had iced the game, that I heard the announcer call, "Interception, Davis. First down, Banning."

Our sidelines erupted.

"It was a touchdown," we were yelling. "You can't take that away. It was six, it was six."

Everybody was jumping and screaming. Coach Knox just hung his head. Lamont and I were running around, trying to figure out how the hell they could rule my touchdown catch an interception.

After that, **things got** *really ugly.* Banning got the ball and ultimately we were assessed 60 yards in penalties. Knox made Lamont and I safeties, figuring we could pick something off because Banning had to score a touchdown to win the game, which meant they had to pass because time was running out. But the refs flagged Lamont for pass interference and a personal foul on one play, I got called for pass interference, and Ronnie

Johnson, one of our linebackers, was so pissed off, he got flagged for a personal foul. Basically the refs just marched Banning down the field. I don't know if the calls were right or not. I knew we were frustrated. Hell, Lamont and I were in tears.

"Man, coach," Lamont said to Knox, "the refs are just giving it away. They're giving it right to them."

He was right and our crowd knew it, too. The game was being played in Gardena, Banning's home field, but, as usual, our side was packed with everyone from *players' families* to *hard-core gang bangers.* Everyone was hot; you could tell something was going to happen.

And when Banning scored to win the game, something did. The final gun sounded and our fans charged out of the stands and started fighting the players, the refs, Banning fans, anyone they could find. We all started fighting, too, swinging helmets, kicking. Skeats was so upset with what had happened that he just took off his helmet and started to walk away.

"Then I saw the fighting," he told me later. "And I strapped my helmet back on and went in swinging."

Unfortunately for Skeats, one of his punches landed upside the head of the Banning athletic director, and it was all caught on video tape. *Big Skeats No. 97, whopping on a little white dude with glasses.* We laugh now, but it was pretty serious back then. The athletic director decided to press charges, and they came and got Skeats out of class the next Monday. He went to court a few times before the A.D. decided to drop the charges. Skeats was suspended from all sports activities for the spring semester—as a participant or as an observer. We still found ways to sneak him in, though. That became one of our specialties.

Three people were arrested during the fight. The police swooped down on the melee in a flash, helicopters flying overhead, their high beams flashing down on us. The game remains pretty famous in L.A. football lore, but it was as bad as I'd ever felt about football. **Cheated** out of a touchdown. **Cheated** out of a chance to play for the city championship.

The funny thing was, I chalked it all up to high school ball and high school refs. I knew it had to be different when I got into the league. Or at least I thought it would be.

The buildup to the Redskins game was kind of fun. The Washington coach, Norv Turner, had been an assistant at USC during John Robinson's first stint there. We got tight. The Jets had considered trying to trade for their quarterback, Gus Frerotte, which meant they would have had to give up the No. 1 pick—me. The Skins wouldn't have taken me, though, because they had drafted a wide receiver, Michael Westbrook, the year before. Actually, that could have been my spot had I come out after my junior year. *It was fun thinking about what might have been* had a few things turned out differently. If Frerotte had gone to the Jets, I'd have been drafted by Jacksonville, which, right now, doesn't sound half bad.

Walking into RFK was cool. So many fans just cutting loose. I saw Chris Hayes, the defensive back we had cut in September. He had been picked up by Washington, which made me happy for him. He can play and I had felt badly when he got cut.

"Man, a brother's got to do what a brother's got to do," he told me when I saw him, thinking I was mad at him because he was playing against us. Chris is one of the few guys I know who could spend five years in rural Washington, playing for Washington State, and still talk like he came right off the streets of South Central. We could have won that Washington game. But taking away my touchdown completely changed the momentum. The Redskins came right back on the next drive and scored to put things away. We were **deflated** emotionally and **frustrated.** We finally had played a good game and now we had to battle the officials, too. It pretty much sucked.

"Key, check out the replay," somebody yelled across the locker room. TNT was showing it again. I looked up and watched along with the entire team and about a dozen reporters who were wanting a few choice words from me about the play.

"Looks like six to me," I said. "If that's not a touchdown, then I don't know what is. I guess I'm just 12 years old out there," I told the reporters. ***"I know if I'm Michael Irvin or Jerry Rice, I get the call.*** But I'm just a pup."

The next day, Kotite revealed that the head of the league officials, Jerry Seeman, told him the call was wrong. We should have had the six points. That didn't make me feel a hell of a lot better. But oh, well. **Welcome to the Jets.**

Of course, once the furor died down, I got a lot of shit from my teammates.

"Damn, Key," big Mo Lewis said one afternoon. "We'd be 4-and-1 if you could just hang on to the ball."

Funny dude, that Mo.

I thought that *game* depressed me. Three days later, I'd know what it really was like to get down. Aaron Glenn and I were going for the ball in one-on-one drills during practice when we both fell, his helmet smacking into the inside of my knee. I heard it pop. I thought it was all over. Ki-Jana Carter, the No. 1 pick the year before me, blew out his knee and missed the entire season. Does bad shit run in twos?

"Shit," I said as I rolled over.

"What do you mean, 'Shit'?" Aaron said, getting up and looking down at me.

I'd never seen a black guy turn green.

"Key, Key," he said, "what do you mean, 'Shit'?"

"I mean, shit, get the trainer," I said. "It's over."

It took a few minutes for the trainer to get to me. By then, everything was in chaos. Thank God no reporters saw what was going on.

I stood up and limped to the training room, feeling my knee swell as I walked. It was the same knee I'd injured during my senior season at USC. At that time, I was going to have it 'scoped between our last regular-season game and the Rose Bowl. But it started to feel better and I cancelled the surgery.

"Key, it looks bad," our trainer, David Price, said. "MRI, now."

So I got into my car and headed for the hospital. I

wasn't really alarmed—I've always been sort of fatalistic about stuff like this. Fortunately, the MRI showed just a slight tear. I thought about not getting the surgery then, just rehabbing it back into shape. But the doctors advised against it, saying if I got hit again, it could tear worse and **then I'd be out for a long, long time.** If I did it now, they said, I'd be back in three to four weeks.

So the next day I headed back to the hospital. I'd never been operated on, hell, I'd never been hurt before, really. My mom reminded me that when I was in Little League, I faked a knee injury because I wanted to see the inside of a hospital. They found nothing wrong and I was sent home before I even made it past the emergency room doors.

This time was different. They wheeled me in and I held my breath. "Make sure you don't slip with the knife," I told the doc.

When it was over and done with, I knew I'd be back sooner than they expected. I'm **young,** I'm **strong,** and I was **going to heal a lot faster** than they thought.

When I went home, they gave me this wild-looking compression bootie, which stretched from my foot to my thigh and was hooked up to a machine. The bootie inflated and stimulated the blood flow in my knee, which helped the healing process.

After four days the only pain I had was from the incision. After five days I was jogging. After six days I was running. ***After a week I was ready to play.*** I had to **sit and suffer** through the Oakland and Jacksonville games, however, and that about killed me. I felt helpless. I don't know if my playing would have changed the outcome of either game, but at least I'd have been doing something besides watching my rehab bag inflate.

Against Oakland we weren't even in the game. Mistakes, bad play-calling, bad execution—we had it all. What I couldn't understand was why they decided, with the score 31–6 in the fourth quarter, to play Jeff Graham, who had also ripped up his knee. They activated him the morning of the game and used him extensively in the fourth quarter, knowing full well we had no chance to win. After the game, Jeff was limping even more than me and was **pissed as hell.**

"Why'd they play you?" Jeff's dad wanted to know. They were standing around his car in the players' parking lot.

"Same reason why they do everything," he answered. *"They don't think. They don't have any idea what they're doing out there."*

"Makes no sense," Mr. Graham said, helping Jeff into his car. "Makes no sense at all."

Two days later the team announced that Jeff would be gone for a month. What a waste.

We got more bad news, too. O'Donnell separated his shoulder on a vicious hit and would be gone four to six weeks. Counting Webster Slaughter (who was also injured in the Oakland game), Jeff, Neil, and me—about $20 million was on injured reserve. Mr. Graham was right. Made no sense.

I think part of the problem was that our practices were soft. At USC we'd go hard for three days, then taper off. Here, we would go soft for three days and taper to nothing. ***Our weight training program was A JOKE:*** I had to call James Strom, the USC strength and conditioning coach, to get some kind of schedule so that I could keep my strength throughout the season. There was hardly any effort at conditioning during the season—it was like they thought we should come to camp in shape (which most guys do these days) and then that would be it. But the body doesn't work that way. When you have soft practices, you need hard conditioning afterwards. We had so many injuries, you had to point to something besides bad luck. ***Even the Jets don't have luck this bad without a reason.***

I stayed home for the Jacksonville game. I would have loved to have played against Kevin Hardy, the linebacker who went No. 2 in the draft. That could have been me. Sometimes I wish it was me. They weren't winning a whole lot of ball games, but they were playing hard and fighting through it. As it was, I was sitting at home watching them on TV.

"Damn, I hate not playing," I said to myself, pounding my couch. "Wayne Chrebet gets 12 catches. If I ever get 12 catches, I'm going to be amazed."

We got up 14–3 early in the game and people in my house started thinking we would get the win.

"Just wait," I said, "There's 2½ quarters to play. Something will happen."

Something did. We fell behind and then Nick Lowery missed a 36-yard field goal that would have pulled us to within a point. We could have been kicking for the win instead of having to go for six on our last possession. ***All that wild stretching and*** *silly working out Lowery does on the sidelines* during practice and the dude, our captain, can't make a 36-yarder. Oh, well—0-and-7.

I started running hard the day of the Jacksonville game and I was going to be practicing on Wednesday, playing on Sunday. **Our season was a mess,** but we still might be able to spoil a few things for people. Buffalo was up. Bruce Smith. Let me at him.

Time-Out

I was in one of my old neighborhoods one day last summer, standing on the corner like I used to when I was younger, talking to a bunch of little Bloods who now rule my streets. My brother Mike happened to drive by, and he stopped to return one of my credit cards that he had used earlier in the day to buy my mother some furniture.

"Hey, can you hook me up with some of those?" one of the little dudes asked me.

"It don't work that way no more," I said, shaking my head. *"This is legit, it ain't stolen. **This is the real deal.**"* The kid just stared at me like he hadn't heard me right. He didn't know me as Keyshawn Johnson, first round draft pick of the New York Jets, soon to be a millionaire. He only knew me as the neighborhood knew me. I'm a legend around there as **a guy who hustled, *PERIOD.***

They don't know anything about me and football, or about me and money. I'm sure his brothers and sisters, and probably his mom, had told him about me and the way it was back when I was running the streets and ruling the corners.

"Man, asking for hot credit cards, you're just looking to get your ass put in jail," I said. The group broke up and the little homies ran off.

Getting shot when I was in junior college was alarming

to me. It showed me that even though I'd started to push myself in the right direction, I was still **vulnerable to the whims of a fool.** But that's always going to be the case, I guess. Mostly what it did was convince me that I needed to stay focused: to get through junior college, make it to USC, and then to the league. That bullet only strengthened my resolve to work harder and to make it.

There was a time, however, that my resolve had nothing to do with working hard or becoming anything other than a kingpin in the neighborhood black market. I was that little dude standing on the street corner trying to make a deal for some **fast, easy money.**

I was never a gang banger, although a lot of my friends were. I didn't get caught up in all that gang stuff because I really couldn't—we moved around too much, from a neighborhood ruled by one gang to a neighborhood ruled by another. My brothers and sisters didn't have it like that—they grew up mainly in a Blood neighborhood and after we all got back together in the same place, we moved to the other side of the tracks, which was ruled by the Crips. It was tough on them, because all their friends were Bloods. *Me, I was too little for anyone to bother with.* I was friends with everybody.

I'd play Little League baseball at Denker Park with a bunch of Bloods, then go home to a place where my friends were enemies of my teammates. In the end, I think my dual life saved me from ever becoming hard-core.

Both sides respected me because I refused to align myself with just one group and because I was an athlete. And I didn't pass judgment. If guys wanted to go gang bang that was fine, just don't go off on me. To this day I can be hanging out with a hundred Bloods and the next day you might see me hanging out with a hundred Crips. Nobody says anything because they know it's just how I am and who I am.

A lot of people don't understand how a kid can avoid being in a gang while growing up in an environment filled with little else. But there are a lot of guys like me who didn't get caught up in all that. You just never hear about them.

Plus, back then I was only interested in **making money.**

By the time I was 13, scalping tickets had become a big operation for my brother Mike and me. During the 1984 Olympics, my mom worked for the Saudi Arabian team, helping them get from venue to venue. They'd give her pins and tickets and she'd then give them to us to sell. I remember she came across some pins from Red China— we had about 20 of them and we sold them for $200 each. This little bitty pin. We had a few Olympic Eagles, too, and only a few of those were made. By the end of the Games, we had grocery bags full of cash. I think we made about $20,000.

After that, we decided to hit the road. We flew to Boston for the 1987 NBA Finals against the Lakers and made a killing scalping tickets. That fall, Mike and I went to Minneapolis for the World Series, arriving a few days before it started. Somehow we hooked up with **Kirby Puckett** and he **gave us about 10 tickets,** which we we sold for **thousands apiece.**

About the only time I remember losing money was the NFC playoffs in 1988. I flew up to San Francisco for the

49ers–Vikings game and it was pouring rain. I stood there for hours trying to get rid of my tickets. I was soaking wet and about to cry because nobody was going to the game. I lost about $500 that day, eating all those tickets.

I got caught by the police a few times, which eventually landed me in juvenile camp. The first time I was arrested was outside the USC–UCLA game at the Coliseum. I had all these player tickets and a lady, a man, and a child came up to me. I thought they were cool because of the kid, but the next thing I knew, they were **slapping CUFFS on me.** Set ups. They took me down to the station and were about to confiscate the money in my pocket, which was around $500. I told them it was my mother's money, that I was supposed to be on my way to pay her bills when I stopped to try to get rid of my game tickets. It really was scalping money, but *they believed me* and *let me go.* I got back in time to watch the game.

Another time I was arrested in Anaheim. Mike and I were scalping tickets to the Angels. The police were on the roof above where we were, watching us the whole time. They sent two guys to buy from us, asking us all kinds of questions about where the seats were. We started to show them on the map when another two guys came up and grabbed us by the arms. We tried to tell them that we were waiting on friends and just trying to get our money back, but they had been watching us and didn't believe any of it. The District Attorney eventually dropped the case, but my juvenile rap sheet was starting to fill out.

It wasn't too long before scalping got old. Some of my

friends ventured into burglary. They started breaking into houses and stealing stuff. But they never really had a plan and a lot of them ended up in jail.

I was the only guy in my group to sell drugs. One of my relatives got me into it, and although I was never a user, I was always a businessman and **I knew a profitable business** when I saw one.

I was never a heavy seller, mainly marijuana and a little rock, but I made a lot of money. After a while, though, the risks got to be too many. I never knew who was coming up behind me or where the police were setting up for their undercover buys. *I did **not** want to go to jail and I did **not** want to die.* Selling drugs promised no protection from either. **I was only 14.**

So I joined in on the burglary business. By then my guys had a ring of things going on, but no direction. I came in and saw how they were doing things, which was wrong, and I started telling them how things should be handled. I guess I became something of **the director.**

It got pretty serious. We made a lot of big-time money, knocking off stores and then selling the stuff on the black market. **I'd target the store** for the break-in and then send the troops out. I'd tell them to wait until the store closed, then smash the windows, back a truck in, and take as much as possible as quickly as possible. I was never directly involved in the actual stealing, but they'd bring me stuff to fence. I was 15 and dealing with guys from all around the world, unloading all kinds of stuff.

On a good night, we'd walk away with $20,000 to $30,000 worth of merchandise. The street value, of course, was far less, but we still made a bunch of money.

You know the movie *Heat*? Al Pacino and Robert De Niro? I was De Niro, and I swear that movie came right out of my head. I wasn't turning over a truck and shooting people for their bearer bonds, but I was the organizer. If the burglary made $100,000 for the guys who pulled it, I'd take $15,000 for myself for setting up the action.

People wonder how I know so much about jewelry. I guess you could say I was in the business for a while. Before the draft, when I had some money, I bought a specially-made **Rolex watch *with diamonds*** encrusted on every link of the band. I hooked up one of my Jets' teammates, Victor Green, with something a little less flashy, too.

The sad thing? I shopped around in the kind of stores we used to rob. What was strange was that the week after I bought the watch, the police called, saying they wanted to take a close look at it. So my agents and I went down the station and let them look it over. Turned out that a witness in a murder case had described the assailant as having worn a similar watch. But my watch was clean—I made sure everything was done right and by the book. I knew people would be coming at me from all directions and **I wasn't about to start dealing in stolen goods again.**

People ask all the time how I'm dealing with all the money. It's actually something I've been preparing for all my life. **I've been there before.** Nobody who knows me now believes that once I started the bad shit, I came into a lot of money. I probably went through a **million dollars *in five years.*** I never invested any of that money. I gambled, bought expensive clothing, cars, went on trips. My mother really didn't know it, but she was living comfortably because I was living as a criminal.

And then I got caught. And somewhere between my first stint in camp and my second, I realized that my future was looking more and more like it would be spent in a cell **in the state penitentiary** than **on an NFL football field.**

The first time I went to a juvenile facility, I was 14. Somebody had given me some stolen tickets to a Who concert at the Coliseum. The guy who owned the tickets reported the theft and the police were waiting. I didn't steal the tickets, I was just trying to scalp them, but the police didn't see it that way. I got a public defender who obviously didn't know what he was doing. He told me to plead guilty, that I'd get probation. Wrong. The judge took a look at my juvenile sheet, filled with arrests for scalping, and **sentenced me** *to six months at Camp Miraloma* on a petty theft charge.

A lot has been written about my camp days. *Sports Illustrated* somehow decided I'd been arrested on gun charges. Other accounts have me arrested for selling drugs. I was never arrested for anything other than scalping stolen tickets. If you don't believe me, look it up. I can't believe all the wrong, dead-wrong shit that makes its way into newspapers and magazines. That stuff can hurt people when it's not true. *Yes*, I did carry a gun sometimes, and *yes*, I did sell a lot of drugs and rob a lot of people, but it was scalping that eventually did me in.

I remember my mother crying as they took me away. *It hurt me a lot to see her so upset.* I didn't think of myself as a threat to society in any sense. I knew what I'd been doing was wrong, but what I got caught for wasn't really my fault. I could see them throwing me in camp for stealing from stores, but scalping stolen tickets? Still, camp had a profound effect on me, mainly because for the first time in my life I had to do what someone else wanted me to do. I wasn't running burglaries anymore and I wasn't running the streets. I was locked up, and I hated it.

About the first person I met at Miraloma was a juvenile probation officer named Murphy Ruffin. Murphy had grown up in the same area of Los Angeles as I had. He had gotten into his share of trouble, but unlike me, nothing he couldn't shake. He was a big, imposing looking dude who had been in some commercials and print ads. Only in L.A. can a probation officer moonlight as a model. Remember the Camel cigarettes commercial from way back, with the black guy with all that curly hair driving a car? That was Murphy.

Murphy and I hit it off real fast. He was **cool** and I liked him a lot more after I saw him on the basketball court. **Dude could *play.*** He told me later that he could see I had some problems, but that I wasn't like the majority of the guys there. He said that probably 75% of them would end up somewhere in the criminal justice system for the rest of their lives. It was the other 25%, he said, that kept him going.

"Key," he'd always say, "make sure you're in that 25 percent."

The camp had two dorms and they were overflowing. We had school every day and got a little time to play ball—mostly hoops. The competition was **fierce,** mainly between guys from different gangs and sets. A lot of fighting went on, guys making weapons out of all kinds of stuff. Someone would get pissed off and eventually his gang would lure the offender around the corner and beat the shit out of him. There were a lot of times **I didn't feel safe there.** Some of those dudes were hard-core. All I knew was that I wanted to do my time and get the hell out.

Murphy and I hung out a lot. He was really into sports, like I was, and we'd sit for hours talking about this game or that team, who was going to do what when. The time passed slowly, though. I couldn't wait to get out, get back with my family.

I stayed out of trouble at Miraloma and, with Murphy's recommendation, got out a little bit early and was placed on probation. By then, my mother and the rest of the kids had moved in with her sister in the San Fernando Valley. There wasn't nearly enough room—at times we had 10 people in a one-bedroom apartment—but my mom thought that by taking me away from the guys I'd been hanging with, she'd be taking me away from trouble. She was partly right. About then *I decided to try to* **CLEAN THINGS UP.** I'd had a taste of being locked up and I had seen too many guys stay there with no hope of turning things around. I stayed away from the group doing the burglaries and I quit selling drugs. I had a pretty sizable bag of cash stashed away with my clothes and I decided to see if I could accomplish all as an athlete that I had as a thief. Murphy talked to me a lot about using **my athletic ability for something positive.**

He was one of the few people who told me early on that I had a real chance of making it in sports.

And I *was* making it in sports, as a member of the Canoga Park High School football team. But making it on a team that was sorry wasn't in my plans and I got frustrated fast. When the season was over and we had won only two games, I'd had enough. I stopped going to class. I'd spend all day lying around at home and then go hang out. Eventually the school found out. When the school found out, my probation officer in the Valley found out. **She hit the ceiling.** We went back to court, where she told the judge I'd violated probation and that she was now recommending I spend the next two years—the rest of high school—at camp.

"This kid has *lied repeatedly* and has done nothing the court required of him," she said. "If he's to amount to anything, he needs to be taught a lesson. We're saying he needs to be in camp until he's 18."

The judge said he would take my case under advisement. And then I was really worried. I couldn't stand the thought of going back for two years. Football would be out of the question, a college scholarship would be *gone.* Everything would be *lost.* My mom suggested I write a letter to the judge explaining my situation. I also got some coaches and counselors to write letters, and in the end, the judge sentenced me to three more months.

"When I see you in my courtroom again in three months," the judge said, "I want to see nothing but grades on that record."

My mother said that she feared I was headed into the regular jail system, that if I didn't straighten myself up, I'd be lost to her for a long, long time. Later, my brother Dennis would be arrested for selling drugs and spend a few years in prison. Mike, somehow, never got caught doing anything, even though he was leading a pretty risky lifestyle for a while. It's funny that I'd be the one of the two of us to do juvenile time. I have to say now, though, the system actually *worked* for me. When I got to the new place, Camp Barley Flats near Mt. Wilson, I realized that I was a step away from hard time. This place was **no joke.** It was summer, so there was no formal schooling. Instead, we were assigned to work crews. We'd head up the mountains, clearing roads, picking up trash, moving dirt and boulders. It was hard work. There was no sports program. We played a little hoops every now and then, but mainly we were too tired and beat up to want to do much else.

Ironically, Murphy Ruffin was transferred to Barley Flats just after I got there. It was about the best thing that happened to me during those years. By then, Murphy and I were tight. I felt bad about letting him down and ending up back in camp, but he never said a word. He has always been positive, telling me that whatever good I put into the world, the more I'll get back. We talked even more about what he called my **God-given talents** and the need for me to pursue them. I had coaches in my life who were positive role models, but ***nobody helped me along the way like Murphy did.*** He wasn't really interested in how many yards I could get or how many catches I could make. ***He was interested in ME.***

"I can set up a beautiful play for you," he'd say. "But you've got to execute it."

The difference between me and the rest of the guys in camp, he told me, was that I had the heart and soul to make the play work.

I went back to see Murphy a few years ago. Barley Flats had since closed down and he was stationed at Camp Scoby. He's still working as a probation officer and is still listening. Of course, he's still talking, too. The last time I talked to him was in October 1996.

"Kotite's gotta go," he said over the phone.

Even a juvenile probation officer at camp in the middle of California could see what I'd been seeing all fall in New York.

When I was released from Barley Flats I decided to try playing ball at Pacific Palisades, and then transferred to Dorsey, where things finally started going right for me. ***I gave up for good the lifestyle of a hood, gave up robbing people, selling drugs.*** All that shit stopped for real. I took a huge pay-cut, but I had had enough of playing dodge ball with the police and the people with the guns.

I had a few more serious run-ins with my old crowd. The summer before my first year at West Los Angeles College, I was hanging out on the corner with a few of the old guys throwing dice. Skeats, my cousin E-Rock, and my brother Mike were with me and a few other guys, including one feisty 12-year-old I'll call Little Louis. We were just **kicking it, gambling a little, talking shit.** I was in the middle of trying to tell Little Louis that he needed to get his ass back to school, but he was hearing none of it. He had about $15,000 in the circle and was fixing on making more.

Some dude came up and asked if we had any rock. We told him to get his ass off the street, that wasn't our thing. I should have known then that he was just scoping us, seeing what kind of money we were playing with. A few minutes later, I see another guy come round the corner with a shotgun and he's cocking it. **"Here come the Crips,"** somebody yelled. "Move, move it."

I thought the dude with the gun could be a Crip because he was all in blue. So I ran up the apartment building stairs to the roof. Little Louis was right behind me and I grabbed him up the last stairs and pulled him up. Meanwhile, the guy with the gun had my cousin cornered in the alley with the **shotgun to his head** and was demanding all the money.

I started screaming from the rooftop.

"We're getting robbed, we're getting robbed. Somebody call the police," I yelled.

I figured someone would come to help us because this was our neighborhood. Instead, I heard a lot of doors slamming and windows closing. I thought E-Rock was gone for sure. Skeats had run and hid behind a big tree, Mike was passed out in his car, too high to know anything was going on. Finally, for some reason, **they let E-Rock go after they took all the money.** Usually they'd just blow the witness away. Little Louis lost a lot of money that night. I lost a little. I don't know if anyone ever retaliated and I don't want to know. I just stayed away from that corner for a while.

I've had guns pointed at me before—when I was 12,

my friends and I stole a bunch of fire extinguishers and were spraying them all over the neighborhood. Some vigilante guy pulled up in a car and called us over. He drew out a big 12-gauge shotgun and held the barrel right on my face. I swear to God it was **cold.** He told us to go home. We did.

Another time I was in an environment that I shouldn't have been in, meaning I was riding with a gang banger who had shot some shit up the night before. A guy rolled up and pointed a gun at the guy I was with, said he was going to kill us both, and then just drove on. **Shit like that happens to guys all the time in Los Angeles.** Now, my position is that if you're gang banging and shooting fools in 1996, then you ought to get shot. You ought to go to jail. I have a daughter now. Lots of people in the inner city have daughters. *We don't need fools driving by our windows, shooting, killing our children.*

I'm still friends with a lot of guys who run with gangs. They were all at my party after the draft, and I still stop and chill with them when I'm in town. That's never going to stop. One thing I am is loyal. As long as they keep me out of the shit they're doing, then they're cool with me. They know my position on gang banging and they respect that. Maybe I'll change some minds, I don't know.

I'm not looking to save people from themselves, but I ain't looking to cut them loose, either.

They're living their lives; I'm living mine. We all make choices.

One night in the spring of 1996, I rolled into New York for a card show and was met at my hotel by a guy from NFL security. They were doing a background check on me, which was cool. I think teams ought to check out who they're getting. I wouldn't want anybody with serious problems on my team.

I had told the NFL all about my past.

"Check all you want. The only thing you're going to find on my record is juvenile stuff for scalping tickets. Ain't nothing else there," I told them.

They came to me in New York, however, not because of my old record. They said they were "concerned" about the character of people I was associating with, the guys I had invited to my party, the gang bangers I know. ***They said they'd placed a red flag by my name.***
"The NFL can't tell me what to do with my life," I told the guys up in my hotel room. "I'm friends with people who gang bang, who sell drugs. That's what they do. I don't do it, but they're my friends. They don't associate their business with me. So if you're asking me to cut them out of my life, I'm not going to do that. You're expecting me to do something I'm not going to do."

They just told me to be careful.

"Shit," I said, "you have no idea who you're talking to, what I've been through in my life."

A lot of young black men in Los Angeles don't ever reach my age. ***I've had friends* killed *and friends* sent up for life.**

There are more black men in the criminal justice system than in college right now. Funeral insurance is a big business in my neighborhood.

I don't need the NFL to tell me to watch my back. I've been doing it all my life.

7

I've never seen people get so fired up over an injury before. **My knee was big news.** Every day there was something in the newspapers about how I was progressing and when I thought I'd be back. People were crazy. Everywhere I'd go guys were saying I should be careful, not rush things.

"Keyshawn," yelled some guy walking down the street in Manhattan. His accent was thick New York. "Hey, man, don't fucking worry about coming back until you're fucking ready."

"Why does everyone keep asking if I'm coming back too soon?" I asked a friend of mine. "I ain't doing nothing to jeopardize my future. I'm ready, that's all there is to it."

So ready, in fact, that on the Wednesday before I ran out for my first practice, I took a Cybex test. It involves lifting weights up and down and laterally with your leg, and it tests the strength of your knee. My knee tested **stronger** than it did before the injury. I sprinted out to the field, ready to ball. Guys went nuts seeing me back out there.

"Can you feel the energy?" I said to Gerry Eskenazi from *The New York Times*.

"I do," he said.

One thing I was not going to put up with was all the bullshit that had been going on before I got hurt. I was sick and tired of the crap the coaches were running and I told Coach Mann, right off, Don't mess with me when I come back. I'd worked too hard in rehab to put up with any mess.

"I don't want no b-s out of y'all," I told him. "I want the fucking ball. I want slants, hitches, and fades. I'm not coming back to clear things out for the other guys. *I ain't* **NOBODY'S** *decoy no more.*" He got my point.

"Don't worry, Key," he said softly, as usual. "We're gonna get you the ball."

And yet, nothing really looked that different my first practice. I got three passes—*three passes*. The next day, I got four passes.

"How's your day going today?" a reporter asked me.

"Well, just great," I said in a mocking voice. "I caught one more pass than yesterday. Maybe tomorrow, if I'm lucky, I'll get five."

On Friday, our last serious day before the Buffalo game, we ended practice by running a drill from our own 20-yard line to the end zone, throwing all passes. I didn't get one ball thrown my way the entire drive. Finally, from the 10, they threw me a fade in the end zone. I caught the damn thing, but **I was still *fairly* disgusted.**

"Hey, you just like Cris Carter," one of our linebackers, Bobby Houston, started yelling at me. Carter's a wide receiver for the Vikings who they say can't catch anything but a fade.

"Cris Carter, Cris Carter—that's it, that's who you are, man," he started yelling.

The whole team was laughing. Pretty soon everyone

was calling me Cris Carter. Telling me Wayne Chrebet, who got all the slants and hitches during the drive, was going to the Pro Bowl. As good as he is, Wayne Chrebet should not be starting on this team. He's a situation guy, *he's* *NOT* *a playmaker.* He has a role, but the coaches need to limit it, use him right. There is no way he should be starting ahead of Alex Van Dyke, but the coaches messed Van Dyke's head up so bad he doesn't know which way to run. First they told Alex he was the man, that his mini-camp was better than mine, and he started thinking he was all it. Then they sat him after he dropped a couple. Then they deactivated him for a game to bring in some miracle-worker kick-return guy who averaged about two yards a return.

Still, Van Dyke is good and he should be starting over Chrebet. Chrebet got you 3–13 and now he was getting you 0–7. Wayne had what, seven more games than us? The kid is gutsy, I'll give him that, and he's reliable, but he's not the guy. Wayne Chrebet—hell, **if he went to the Pro Bowl, it would be a damned conspiracy.**

"Erhardt," I said disgustedly to Webster Slaughter after practice when we were both getting treatment in the training room. "Running that bullshit stuff, giving me one pass on a drive. I can't figure him out. He didn't say one word to me when I was injured, not 'How are you doing?' Didn't poke his head in here once to even say hello."

"I tell you one thing," Webster said, "I'm gone after this season. Ain't no way I'm coming back to play for that man."

I didn't think there was one guy on this team who wanted to play for Erhardt. I knew that if **Kotite**

went and **Erhardt stayed,** there would be a mutiny—I could guarantee it.

We were loose, yeah. We were 0–7 but most of us knew we weren't gonna get fired. It was the coaches and management who were getting tight. And Steve Gutman wasn't smiling about nothing. He had to be tearing his hair out.

"Stay strong, stay strong," he told me one day after practice.

"Hey, I'm black every single day."

He just looked at me, pretty shocked. He didn't know how to respond to that one.

And our running backs coach, Richard Wood? He looked like he was going to go into cardiac arrest at any moment. Even Mike Kensil, who calls himself the director of operations, although ***I've never seen him do a lick of work,*** got hot at my buddy Tamecus for cutting players' hair in the locker room.

"We can't be having this anymore," he told Meek as he was giving Richie Anderson a cut. "It causes too much of a mess and it's a distraction. You shouldn't be in here."

"Hey," Richie said, "Meek's cutting my hair now and he's going to do it next week, too. You don't sweat the white guys when they shave, they cause just as much mess."

I heard about it and went crazy.

"Leave my friends alone," I told Kensil. "This is my guy, and he's going to cut hair for anybody who wants him to."

The whole organization was **scared as hell.** Saturday nights before games we had an 11 o'clock curfew. The coaches came around knocking on our hotel doors to make sure we were inside. I was getting off the elevator at about 11:05 the night before the Buffalo game and our offensive line coach, Bill Muir, was standing there with steam coming out his ears.

"This is a fine, you know," he said to me.

"You ain't touching one dime of my money," I said back. "Hey, we're 0–7 and you're worrying about me being five minutes late?"

He glared at me as I turned and walked down the hallway. I knew he was pissed. Oh, well. He probably wouldn't be around for long anyway.

There was some other wild stuff going on, too, besides the goofy shit the coaches were pulling. Rumblings about the **bounty on my head** were starting to get pretty loud. I'd never taken this shit seriously, but other people were starting to notice.

Like I said before, I had heard all the noise in August about some dude from the Chiefs wanting to pay somebody on the Raiders $150,000 to take me out during our preseason game. And then people started hearing that the bounty was on for our regular-season game against Oakland, which I ultimately didn't play in because I hurt my knee the Wednesday before the game.

Fred Edelstein reported on a threat against me in his little weekly newsletter. And about a week later a sportscaster from Los Angeles I know gave my agent similar information.

"You know people around the league ***aren't lik-ing*** *how* ***Keyshawn's acting,*** what he's saying," the sportscaster told my agent, Jerome Stanley.

We called the NFL to let them know what was going on; everybody from Paul Tagliabue on down was scrambling to find out if any of this shit was true. NFL security started calling everyone to see who was the source of the information. A guy named Q. Williams was assigned to the case and he was saying the NFL was furious about the situation. They investigated the rumors and in the end found no basis for any of them.

Still, I thought it was **pretty funny.** Deion Sanders had warned me during my party after the draft that a lot of guys were going to hate me and be out to make sure I failed, or at least ended up in traction.

"There're a lot of player haters in this league," he said.

I went out with Charles Barkley after the Rockets played the Knicks in New York. He laughed, too, when I told him the story.

"Shit, they just **jealous because they ain't you,**" he said. "Keep on doing what you're doing. Ain't nobody gonna touch you."

Barkley also told me I wasn't going to win until we got rid of Kotite. The two had overlapped in Philadelphia when Barkley played for the 76ers.

"He sucked then, too," Barkley said. "Get rid of him and be your own man, you'll be fine."

What none of these people knew about was a run-in I'd had with Buffalo's Bruce Smith during the Super Bowl in January. I was in Phoenix partying and he was in Phoenix partying and we both happened to be partying at the same club on the same night. Bruce was faded, *a few too many Mai Tai's,* I think. He was all glassy-eyed and slurry, but came up to me and got right in my face.

"Rookie," he said, "when we play next fall, I'm going to break your fucking jaw."

And then he just started laughing hysterically, like some crazy man. After a few seconds, we all started laughing, too.

"You ain't even gonna be near my ass," I told him. "I'm going to run so fast right by you, **I'll be a blur.**" Sterling Sharpe, formerly of the Green Bay Packers and now with ESPN, was standing there laughing, too.

"Hey, he all right," he said to Bruce about me.

"Yeah, he all right," Bruce slurred back. "But I'm still going to get his young rich ass."

By game-time against the Bills, **I was pumped—** Bruce Smith or no Bruce Smith. I doubted he'd even re-member the conversation. It just felt good to be back out there on the field getting ready for a big one on a Sunday afternoon. It seemed like I'd missed more than two games. I hated watching those two debacles, and I was determined to come back with fire in my legs and in my heart. Frank Reich was at quarterback, which, to me, was good news. Reich knows who to throw to.

"Put the ball in my hands," I told Kotite on the field. **"We can win this bitch."**

"You're damned right," he said back.

I was feeling it as they announced my name over the loudspeaker and I high-stepped through the line, high-fiving guys and screaming like a girl. I wanted to play. I wanted to win.

First series we were smoking. Ol' boy Erhardt decided

to establish the running game. A novel idea. But it was working. We moved the ball to midfield and on first-and-10, I went in motion against Jeff Burris, a third-year guy out of Notre Dame, and burned him bad for 18 yards. And then just to make sure he noticed, I burned him again for 16 yards into the end zone. Touchdown.

Man, it felt good. I caught the pass, squeezed it tight, then **spiked it *hard* and pointed to my right knee.** I wanted the whole damn stadium and the millions watching at home (well, O.K., the thousands at home) to know that my knee was strong, my attitude was strong, and that I was back.

"See, I told you, I told you," I yelled at Kotite when I ran back to the sidelines.

"Damn right," he said.

"Baby," big Marvin Washington yelled, "we're rolling now."

We were. It was the first time all season that we had scored on our first drive of the game. Hell, I think it was probably the first time in two seasons that the Jets had scored on their first drive of the game. I thought we'd take it to them again, too, on the second drive, except that the guy I burned on the first drive, Burris, didn't like getting burned.

On third-and-16 from the Bills' 24-yard line, Reich zinged a beautiful pass right at me, about 15 yards upfield. Burris made a wonderful play, though, grabbing my arms just as the ball hit, and the ball fell to the ground. Then, our illustrious field-goal kicker, Nick Lowery, managed to hit the right upright from 43 yards, and we came away with nothing. The Bills had scored on a 48-yard field goal the possession before and would score another field goal the next time they got the ball. We blew one.

"Time for Nick to go," I said to Van Dyke on the sidelines. **"Dude needs to be cut.** They should be saying, 'Nickie, we let you break the record [alltime field goals], we love you, goodbye.' "

Even the fans were booing.

The two-minute warning before halftime sounded and we had one more chance to try to get some points on the board. We started from our own 21-yard line. Reich, out of the shotgun, launched one right into the waiting hands of tight end Tyrone Davis, who proceeded to drop the ball.

"Don't be dropping the motherfucking ball," I yelled at Davis as we ran back to the line. "We needed that one."

On third-and-10, Reich found me for 14 yards, giving us a first-and-10 on our own 37-yard line. Things were moving. We still had time. And then Reich threw to Davis again, but the ball glanced off his fingertips and into the hands of the Bills. I made the tackle, the first of my professional career. Tyrone wouldn't even look at me.

The Bills missed a 36-yard field goal off of that turnover, but we only led by 7–6 at halftime. They weren't scoring the TDs, but **they were shoving the ball right down our throats,** mainly on the strength of running back Thurman Thomas, who, during the course of the game, broke the Bills' career rushing mark of 10,186 yards, set long ago by O.J. Simpson.

A lot of people have asked me whether I thought O.J. was guilty. The news media came at me and my USC teammates in droves after the murders, trying to get us to say something—anything—about our fellow Trojan. It got pretty crazy on campus. Somebody stole Simpson's jersey out of the case in Heritage Hall, and the sports information department had to run people off all the time. We got the word from our coach, John Robinson, on what to say.

"No comment."

That was pretty easy.

When the murders happened we were all pretty shocked that O.J. was a suspect. **The Juice was cool.** But as I said to my friends then and as I say now, I wasn't there, I didn't see who killed those people, so I don't have an opinion one way or the other.

I did, however, see O.J. on the 405 freeway during his little drive back to his house. A couple of guys and I jumped in a friend's car and worked our way up the highway until we were **right next to the Bronco.** I'd met Al Cowlings before, and A.C. just looked over at us and kind of smiled. I figured O.J. was in the back seat, but I didn't know until later that he had a gun to his head. We just wanted to see what was going on.

The trial made the city crazy. Some said it caused a bigger split between black people and white people in Los Angeles, but **I don't see how the split could get much bigger.**

It made me think a lot about what was going on with my own race and how we were treating each other—gangs vs. gangs, black-on-black killings.

The O.J. thing also made me think about interracial relationships, and why people still trip over them. I'm friends with a lot of white women and I'm friends with a lot of black women. The mother of my daughter is half black and half Chinese. I think you love who you love, regardless of their skin color. But I also think people need to stay true to themselves and who they are and where they come from. I can yuk it up with white, corporate America without selling out the blackness in me. **O.J. was a sellout.** *He tried to get away from his blackness.* That's something I'll never do. I am black and I am strong. I'm not a racist and I don't hate anyone, except people who hate me for being who I am. Racism is a volatile issue—especially in Los Angeles. I think about it a lot.

All I knew heading into the second half against the Bills was that we had to find some way to stop O.J.'s successor. **Thurman Thomas is a class guy** with a wicked ability to run the ball. He had to be getting tired, I kept thinking. Damn, the guy'd been running on just about every play. The second half started, and finally we got the break we needed.

The Bills had recovered one of our fumbles—Richie Anderson got a bad handoff from Reich—and on the next play we recovered one back and were sitting first-and-10 on the Bills' nine-yard line.

"O.K., Key," Reich said to me as we huddled up. "C'mon, let's go."

The play was the same one we had used against the Redskins, when I scored but they gave the defender the interception.

"I'm not letting him take the ball this time," I was saying to myself as I pulled it in for six. "Not this time."

We got the TD and made the two-point conversion and things were looking really, really good. We were up 15–9 and all the fans were on their feet. The place was *popping.* Fans are funny, though. They bust me up. Especially the ones right behind our bench. Yelling all kinds of crazy shit. They don't know it, but we hear just about everything they say.

"Kotite sucks," seemed to be the most popular chant. Or, "Get rid of Erhardt," even, "Keyshawn, go in on defense." Usually we just laugh. One time, though, a dude got my attention.

"Hey, Keyshawn, go hit Kotite in the head for me."

I turned, looked back at the guy, then walked over behind Kotite and acted like I was actually going to do it. I looked back again and **the dudes were rolling in the aisles.**

I gave them a thumbs-up sign.

"Keyshawn," they yelled, toasting me with their cups of beer. "You're the man."

With 10 minutes left in the game we were still ahead, but only by 15–12 after the Bills kicked another field goal. Damn, Steve Christie had a good foot. But we had the ball and we were moving it so well, I was thinking we'd score again and win. And then Reich got a bad snap and fumbled on our own five-yard line. Erhardt went psycho, especially after the Bills took it in for six and regained the lead.

"What the hell happened?" he kept asking Reich. "Was

the ball wet? Did it slip?" **Who cares what the hell happened,** I was thinking. It happened, move on, quit worrying about why. But Erhardt just couldn't let it go. Two possessions later he was still asking Frank if the ball was wet. I had to say something.

"Hey, we're trying to win the game here," I told him. "It doesn't matter how it happened. It's over, it's over."

As I was talking I was watching our defensive line get blown off the ball. The Bills were moving and it was killing me. Jim Kelly hit Andre Reed for a 10-yard pass to give them a first down. Victor Green, one of our cornerbacks, was on the coverage and tackled Reed, both of them falling to the ground. Green got up and then turned and helped Reed up.

"Y'all too nice," I was screaming at him. "That's what's wrong with this team, y'all too nice. **Don't be helping that motherfucker up.**"

Next time Victor hit Reed, he let him lie. Attitude. That's what we needed.

Unfortunately, on our last drive Frank had thrown another interception. He was aiming for me but left it short, and I didn't have enough time to turn back and get it. Burris stepped in again, grabbed the ball, and the Bills scored another field goal—now they were up 22–15 with 3:02 left in the game.

"My fault," Frank said on the sideline. "I should have just aired it out."

"If you're going to leave it short," I said, "leave it way short to give me some room."

"I just should have let it rip," he said.

"Let's do it now," I answered, and we ran back on the

field, ready for what I would later consider the best drive all year. We had 2:54 left in the game and the ball on our own 20-yard line. We drove up the field with a no-huddle offense, moving the ball on passes to me and to Chrebet.

"You've got to throw to Wayne," I told Frank after he threw at me when I was covered by about five guys. "If five guys are on me, somebody's got to be open."

I got hit hard a lot during that game. One time Chris Spielman nailed me so hard that **I saw white,** and all I heard for a few minutes was a hum in my ears.

"Damn, that guy can hit," I said later.

So Frank took my advice and started looking for Chrebet, and Chrebet was there. At the two-minute warning we talked about what we needed to do. The ball was on the Buffalo 36 and we had a first down.

"End zone, end zone," I was saying.

"Okay, look for it," Erhardt said to Frank.

Frank dropped back and zinged one at Chrebet. Incomplete, but we got a break that saved our collective asses: a roughing-the-passer penalty on Matt Stevens. That moved the ball to the 21, and it was still first down. Frank had two incompletes to Chrebet, but on third down threaded *one of the* **BEST PASSES** I've seen right into the little guy's hands, for a touchdown. Chrebet was double-covered and later told us he closed his eyes and somehow the ball ended up in his hands as he was sliding across the turf on his back. His arms were pretty skinned up, turf burns and all, but we were tied and we knew—I knew—we were going to OT. What I didn't realize was that there was 1:43 left on the clock, and that ended up being *just enough time for Jim Kelly* **to do his thing.**

Victor Green nearly made an interception that would have sent the game to OT. But on second down from our 37-yard line, **the Bills called a gutsy, gutsy play:** Thurman Thomas up the middle. Nobody was looking for it and he scooted through for eight yards to help set up a field goal, which gave the Bills the win.

I was stunned. The whole team was stunned. Green and another DB, Gary Jones, were lying on the ground, unable to move. We had played so well, especially on our last drive. Kotite called it "a damned shame."

"I'm tired of this shit," I told Jeff Graham outside the stadium. Jeff was on injured reserve for the game, but had limped along with us to the players' parking lot. **"What do we have to do to get a win?** This is serious. I don't know what else to do."

"Just wait," he said, and smiled. "I'll be back next week."

Big Darick Holmes from the Bills walked out and came over. D and I go back to high school days. He played at John Muir High School in Pasadena when I was at Dorsey. Then he went to Portland State and had made it big-time with the Bills. I hated losing to him.

We started talking trash, laughing at each other.

The players' parking lot after a game is usually a happening place to be. All the women—girlfriends, wives—stand around eyeballing each other, checking each other out. The families are usually around, too. Mainly us players give each other a rough time. It's still kind of fun, though. I can't imagine what it would be like if we walked out there as winners.

Holmes was **giving me grief** because he had heard some bullshit that I had guaranteed we'd stomp the Bills. Len Berman at Channel 4 was spreading it around. I never, ever guaranteed that we'd beat Buffalo. I said we'd win sometime, that we wouldn't go 0–16, but I guess people took it wrong. Even in L.A. on my home radio station, 92.3 The Beat, they were giving me shit for guaranteeing a victory when they said I had no right to. I never did. **I ain't that stupid.**

It was a good game for us. Some reporter asked if there was a moral victory to be had because we had come so close.

"Moral victories don't get you a W in the column that counts," I answered. "That's all that counts."

Still, I was feeling a lot better about my role on the team. I was playing with confidence and was more relaxed than ever. Until then, really, I'd been worrying about how much they were going to play me, when I'd be used. All kinds of bullshit that I didn't need to be concerning myself with. I think they were realizing they had to get me the ball. I told Erhardt during the game to quit running the counter, stick with the slants. He actually listened to me a couple of times.

And, believe it or not, I was starting to think that maybe Kotite wasn't such a bad guy. I still thought he had to go—that wouldn't change—but I started to think it was the guys around him who were screwing us and him up. He had some lame assistants, his old-boy crew from Philadelphia. He even had one assistant, a little ass-kisser fat dude, who collected fines when we made mistakes at practice. *At practice.* We got fined if we jumped offsides, if we dropped a pass or fumbled. I've never heard of fines for mistakes at practice.

At least I knew that Kotite wanted to win. He's a fighter, ***one of those old boxer dudes*** who won't let his guard down. I think that if he had gotten rid of Erhardt and some of those other old fools, given some power to guys like Coach Mann and the tight ends coach, Pat Hodgson, then we might have won a few by then. But at 0–8, all their asses were tight and I didn't know what in hell was going to happen next.

We had one, maybe two, games before the $25 million man was supposed to come back. But I hoped he wasn't in any hurry. Frank Reich is a better quarterback. He's more patient and **he isn't looking to protect his stats.** Frank said, I'm just going to throw it in front of me, it's up to you guys to come down with it. And, for the most part, we did.

The problem was, this team didn't know how to win yet. When it came down to the fourth quarter we were giving in, expecting the worst to happen. All we had to do was stop Thurman Thomas behind the line, or sack Jim Kelly, or do something so that we weren't in a situation where it was do-or-die in the last two minutes. When we got past all that, then we would start winning. I felt like we were close, but you never knew.

We got one. Finally.

I can't remember when I have felt so desperately relieved after a victory. We beat a sorry team in our 31–21 win over the Cardinals, but we didn't care. It was a W, and to us—to me—it was a big one. Hell, judging by the atmosphere in the locker room after the game you'd have thought we had won the damn Super Bowl.

Everybody was hollering and laughing, cracking jokes. A *loud, rowdy* locker room. A winning locker room.

"Keyshawn, you did it for us," Kotite said to me when we ran off the field after the final seconds ticked off the clock. **"I should have listened to you earlier.** I should have gotten you the ball. You've showed me a lot. We're gonna get you the ball from now on."

I was sort of shocked to hear those words from Kotite. Damn, the dude was sweating and everything. I think his butt must have been on the line for this game—on the hot-seat. You know, win or bye-bye? I can't imagine why else he looked so drained and was admitting something I'd been telling him since day one.

He told the team he was as proud of us as any team he'd ever coached.

"When I go into the trenches," he said, "I want you all with me."

Whether or not we would follow, well, that was another story. One win meant nothing except that now we didn't have to worry about going 0–16. All week long the press had been dogging me about my supposed guarantee that we'd beat Buffalo. Now I gave them a little back.

"I'll go out on a limb with you folks," I told them, "and guarantee that we'll win again this season."

I thought we would.

The whole week leading up to the game had a special feel to it. That's why I thought all along we'd beat Arizona. On Tuesday, October 22, our day off before the Arizona game, I spoke at the Four Seasons Hotel at a fancy luncheon for a group of people from a magazine called *React*, a spin-off of *Parade*, the magazine a lot of people get with the Sunday paper. There were about 100 people there, mostly middle-aged, **all white.** My man Tamecus and I provided the contrast.

I was invited along with women's hoops star Rebecca Lobo, gymnast Amy Chow, and the biggest swimmer I've ever seen, Tom Dolan. All of us, in one way or another, had overcome obstacles to get where we were, and I guess the magazine was trying to help kids today do the same thing. I didn't see any kids in the audience, just a lot of potential advertisers. But oh, well, that's business.

The food was fancy as hell and I was starving—and that was after we ate. The limo driver and I had been joking on the way into the city from Long Island.

"You know it's going to be small—the higher the price, the smaller the portions," the guy said.

"Yeah," I said. ***"Some circle of weird fish and two grains of rice."***

I wasn't far off. Too many forks, too. Tamecus and I just kind of stared at them and made a guess as to which one we were supposed to use. We started laughing, saying somebody in the back, probably a brother, had to wash **100 plates** and about **6,000 forks.**

Lobo talked about her mother's breast cancer and Dolan talked about his asthma. Chow didn't say much— I'm still not sure what it was she had to overcome— maybe being short. And then it came time for me to talk.

"Adolescence is adolescence," I said. "You're going to run around breaking car windows and all that ... "

Everybody started chuckling. A funny thought, any of them breaking car windows.

"But you can do those things and turn out O.K. Look at me—I got into a lot of trouble, but I got out. Hopefully one day we'll win some football games ... "

More laughter.

" ... and then I'll be successful in New York. Today's society is kind of wild, you've got to keep things on the positive side."

They gave me a **standing ovation,** like I was some political candidate or something. Then came the questions. Somebody asked what we did in our free time.

"I try to get far away from swimming," Dolan said. "Get my mind off it and as far away from the pool as I can."

"I'd like to get away from the Jets," I said, and everyone started laughing again. "That'd make my life a whole lot easier."

Later, somebody said I'd charmed white, corporate America. If I did, I did it by just being myself and using whatever the hell fork I wanted to.

A day earlier, David Shula had been fired at Cincinnati and Jim Mora had resigned at New Orleans. I wondered what was going to happen with Kotite. We all wondered. Mora is a very, very good coach, but he just kind of lost it after they got beat by Carolina, saying his team sucked. Well, he was right. They did suck. He's still a good coach though. Somebody said Terry Donahue, the former coach at UCLA, was being considered for the job. He's good, too, he can get the job done.

I could play for Donahue. I could play for a lot of people. John Robinson—he could get it done in New York. That would be wonderful. Mike Ditka would be a good coach. A lot of people think he's a hard-line, washed-up, schizo-type guy. Probably he is, but I still think he can coach. I'd even play for the cowboy-boot guy, Jerry Glanville, or Buddy Ryan. I'd be best friends with somebody like Buddy Ryan. *I'd let Buddy be Buddy and he'd let me be me.*

Leave each other alone, play ball, win games. It's not that hard to figure out. I could play for Bill Parcells, and I hear he is unhappy at New England. Hell, I'd love to play for Parcells. He's tough and he knows how to win. Playing for Parcells would be wonderful.

The biggest mistake the Jets could make after this season, besides not firing Kotite and Erhardt, would be to hire someone without talking to us players first. They need to find out who we want, who we think can best lead us. Gutman never played any ball. **He's a bean-counter.** Who's closer to the game than the players? You think management didn't talk to Jordan or Bird or Magic before they brought somebody in? Hell, Magic got Paul Westhead fired because he didn't like him. I'm not saying that I'm in the same league as those athletes—not yet. But we've got nowhere to go here but up. And if Leon Hess, or whoever's in charge, doesn't call me come hiring time, you know I'll be calling him.

Stuff on the field was pretty intense during the week. We knew the Cardinals were sorry—they knew it, too. Most of us were thinking that if we couldn't beat Arizona, then we were a long way off from where we thought we were.

We've got some talent on this team. We're not deep—get past our first string and just about any college baller could make our team. The problem is not the players or even playing for the Jets. It's the coaches. Not just Kotite. Maybe not Kotite at all. His assistants, though, man, they're messed up.

After the Buffalo game, our offensive line coach, Bill Muir, pulled Coach Mann aside to talk about me. He told Mann that I had been "too hard" on the linemen during the Buffalo game and that I should lay off because it was pissing some of them off. When Coach Mann repeated this to me, **I BLEW UP and walked**

right up to Muir's face. He hadn't counted on that.

"What the hell do you mean, I was too hard on the O-Line?" I asked him. He just stared back at me, glaring.

"What I said during the game was trying to **get their big asses out there to block** for Adrian and keep Frank from getting sacked," I told him. "Nobody had a problem with it. They said, 'Yeah, yeah, let's go.' You got a problem with that, then you got bigger problems than anyone knows."

Kotite overheard me yelling at Muir.

"What's this?" he said, walking over.

Coach Mann told him.

"Yeah, I was cussing, hollering, telling them to block, block, let's go, let's go," I said. "That's called being a team leader."

Kotite shook his head in agreement.

"Leave my guy alone," he said to Muir and walked away.

I turned, too, and headed into the locker room. I felt Muir's eyes on the back of my head.

"O-linemen might get mad," I said, shaking my head. **"Hell, I hope they do get mad.** We're 0–8, what is he tripping about?"

Our PR director, Frank Ramos, came by my locker and told me his phone had been ringing off the hook.

"We got people calling saying you should go in on defense, too," he said.

"Sure, pay me double, I'll play D," I said, laughing.

By game time against Arizona I was pretty nervous

about what was going to happen. Mainly, **I was just praying that we wouldn't blow this one,** and that Frank Reich would just get the ball to me.

But it was great to be back in the sunshine and close to California. And I was finally getting a chance to play at Sun Devil Stadium. I'd been there before, watching Lamont play there in the Fiesta Bowl when Colorado took on Syracuse, and a few other games. But I had never played there myself.

My whole crew was there from Los Angeles. My mom and all my sisters piled into a couple of cars and made the eight-hour drive. Other guys flew. The night before the game was like a big ol' family reunion. Everyone was pretty pumped up. They figured we had a chance to win this one.

And we did. Right off things were working, flowing right. Nick Lowery made a field goal and then Erhardt made a great call, a flea-flicker pass to me in the end zone. I couldn't have been more wide open, and suddenly we were up 10–0. Then came a play that made me think maybe we really were starting to get an attitude. Adrian Murrell was running all over the Cardinals defense. During the second quarter, he got tackled, but when he got up he stepped right on Seth Joyner's stomach. Joyner got up swinging and got thrown out of the game. *We were **laughing** and **cheering** so hard I thought I'd bust apart.*

"Way to show that dog," I yelled when Adrian came back to the huddle. "That's one out the game, let's get another."

Everyone was getting into the act, even little Chrebet. He caught a pass for a first down, then stood there and signaled first down with his arms just for the fans, who were booing.

"Keyshawn's rubbing off on everyone," the TV announcer, Randy Cross, said.

I was just hoping that the Jets history wouldn't rub off on me. The Cardinals came close to catching us—I knew that was inevitable—but we stood strong. Especially in the fourth quarter. That's when we had buckled in the past. This time, it wasn't going to happen. I wasn't about to let Arizona, or even the officials, take this one from us. But things got scary. Murrell fumbled and Arizona ended up scoring a touchdown off the turnover. Suddenly the score was 17–14.

"If the Jets blow this lead, *hide all sharp objects from Richie Kotite,*" Cross was saying on the tube.

No shit. Hide them from me, too.

We scored on our next possession, taking the ball 90 yards. We were methodical, consistent, and we made the drive work. But all that was wiped out on the kick return, when the Cardinals' Leeland McElroy ran the ball 92 yards. Two plays later the Cardinals scored. As you might imagine, I had a few **choice words** for the special teams guys.

And then it was time for our big play. Murrell burst up the sideline and took off like a lightning bolt, running 78 yards before he was pulled down at the two-yard line. Reggie Cobb scored to make the lead 31–21 and then, in the final minutes, our DB Lonnie Young intercepted a pass in the end zone. Game over. We got the W.

"Make sure you get a shot of the scoreboard," I told all the photographers as we ran off the field. "First win! First win!"

The locker room was crazy, people screaming, laughing. I don't know the last time I've been so happy. Probably not since the Rose Bowl in January 1996, when USC beat Northwestern. We started in on Murrell for running out of gas and getting caught before he could get in the end zone.

"Man, you got reeled in," Mo Lewis yelled from the training room. He had torn a chest muscle which, we'd find out the next day, would knock him out for the rest of the season. *"Adrian, that boy* sucked you up *like a vacuum cleaner."*

Murrell just laughed.

"You'd better be out running tomorrow," I joked with him. "Don't be getting caught like that again, embarrass the whole team."

I *was* joking—it was a beautiful run and it put the seal on a wonderful victory.

Everyone was really happy. My family was bouncing outside the locker rom when I came out. There were hundreds of people waiting around, asking for autographs. **I just wanted to hug my baby and my mom,** but my sister Sandra wouldn't hear of it.

"These people came to see you and you entertained them the whole game," she said. "Now, *GO SIGN* **their books."**

She was right. I started laughing at her, then I started signing. And signing.

Since we had the bye week coming up, I got special permission from Kotite to fly straight to Los Angeles, rather than back to New York with the team and then to L.A. For once, the coaches were thinking logical stuff. I kind of wish, though, that I could have been with the team for the trip back. I guess the plane was hopping.

Instead, I jumped on a flight with a couple of my homeboys and headed home—to my real home. From the airport, we drove right to the Century Club—the best place to go in Los Angeles on a Sunday night. You'd have thought I had just come home from battle, **a conquering hero.**

The women suddenly thought I was finer, the guys thought I was cooler. The same club bouncer who a year ago wouldn't let me in because I had on the wrong clothes, was ushering me to a private, reserved table stocked with champagne.

Being a celebrity is **cool.** But winning makes everything **better.**

 **PATRIOTS 31**............**Jets 27**

Being back in Los Angeles during the bye week was real cool. Sunshine, warm weather, my family all around, my daughter falling asleep on my chest. *Life was feeling* $GOOD.$ I spent my time catching up with everybody, seeing my boys, coaches, ex-teammates. You name it. I felt like I'd just gotten out of juvenile detention camp all over again.

I had four days until I had to be back in New York and I was going to make the most of them. One of the first things I did was something very important to me—not something I wanted publicity or attention for. It wasn't like that. What I did was *hand out a* **bunch** *of* *checks* to folks who had been with me and helped me along my way. I had already given money to my sisters and brothers and aunts and cousins. I did that the first week I got paid. And my mom and Shikiri and the baby are well taken care of every month. Now it was time to say thanks to people who had **been there when I had** **NOTHING** and didn't care if I ever got rich, as long as I stayed straight. People like Skeats's mom, Everett, and Roz Hairston, whose house I hung out at a lot (and still do) and whose daughters are like sisters to me. They always had something on the stove for me when I'd come by in high school and never fussed about me hanging out week after week. They always said the couch had my name on it. I promised myself then that if I ever did make it to the league, I wouldn't forget who helped me get there.

There were others, too. A few weeks earlier I had been a guest on a Los Angeles TV show called *Monday Night Live*, which follows *Monday Night Football* on the local ABC affiliate. They hooked me up from New York over satellite and I spent about 30 minutes talking with the host, Todd Donahoe.

When I got home from the studio I got a call from Tank, one of the boys I hung out with growing up. Tank had always been loyal to me.

"I saw you, Key," he said. "I saw you on the TV in that grown man's suit."

When I was home I went and saw Tank, too.

I also called my old coach at West Los Angeles College, Rob Hager, and told him to get his team together and get down to Planet Hollywood on Wednesday night—**dinner was on me.** You mention free food to anybody in junior college—even the coaches—and I'll guarantee a big crowd. I remembered how hungry I got during those days and I knew those guys were struggling, too. Staying straight, on the right path—especially at a junior college in Los Angeles—is a very tough thing to do. I wanted to give them all a break, and *give something back* to Hager and all his assistants, like Darryl Holmes, who had helped me get my act together.

"There aren't a lot of guys who come back," Hager told a friend of mine later. "You can still touch Key. You can still shake his hand, slap him upside the head. There aren't many superstars who stay the same and give something back at the same time."

I gave the football program $12,000, which it really needed. I hope they buy some new weights for that rickety old weight room.

I also called Richard Almeraz, a guy who had been writing me letters since my first year at USC. He was always telling me to hang in there, stay positive; he claimed all along that he was my biggest fan. I invited him to the Planet Hollywood dinner, too, and made him the official first member of my fan club and gave him a bunch of stuff. **That man was so happy,** I couldn't believe it.

Helping kids, especially kids in the inner city, is something I have wanted to do for a long time. I never took drugs or did any drive-bys, but I knew a lot of people who did. I did some bad stuff, but everyone I knew was doing it, too. I know I can help some guys now, just by talking to them about what I went through. If a guy's serving time for a double murder, it's too late. But there are a lot of others out there who can be helped. I know I'm going to be doing my part.

I flew back to New York Thursday afternoon, barely making the October 31 be-back-or-be-fined deadline. I guess the coaches wanted us back before the weekend began to make sure we all weren't running wild in our hometowns. Like that was going to hurt our win-loss record. We had a pretty hard practice on Friday and Saturday and then we were off until Monday morning. To me, that meant *it was time to* **have a little fun**—*East-Coast style.* So I hired a limo and took Wayne Chrebet, Henry Bailey, and Jeff Graham and his brother to Atlantic City to do some gambling. People were surprised that I invited Chrebet, but I got nothing against Chrebet. It's not his fault that he's *loved* by the entire coaching staff and **gets all the passes.** But I was sort of surprised that he wanted to go.

We played craps well into the night. I have to say the trip was fun as hell, except that I lost a lot of money. Way too much money.

"How much?" Tamecus asked when I got back.

"$4,700," I said glumly.

"That's not bad," he said.

"Now there you go, sounding like Shikiri, thinking $4,000 ain't a lot of money," I said. "Just because I make a lot of money doesn't mean that $4,700 don't mean something to me."

I was sick. Really sick. **I hate losing money.**

"I ain't going back there for a long, long time," I said. "That place makes me sick."

"Man, you make it sound like you lost $20,000," Tamecus said.

We had practice on Monday, starting to get ready for the Patriots—**our next victim. HAH.** That sounded funny. I was still tired from the gambling junket, so I went to bed early to get some good sleep. Or so I thought. The phone rang at 1:30 in the morning.

"Hello?" I said, ready to cuss out whoever was calling.

"Key, it's Kobe. What's up?"

Kobe Bryant from the Lakers, a very cool kid yeah, but a very unwise kid, calling me at 1:30 in the morning to see if I wanted to come out to the clubs in New York City. The Lakers had just gotten into town for a Tuesday night game against the Knicks.

"Nah, man, I'm asleep," I said.

"No, c'mon, Key, I need you. They're saying I can't get in to the China Club."

The China Club is the hot place to go on Monday nights.

"What do you mean, you can't get in?" I asked.

"They carded me, man. I ain't got no I.D."

I forgot, the little man was **only 18 years old.**

"Don't you know somebody here who can get me in?" he was asking.

"Why don't you go with Shaq and them?" I asked.

"Aw, man, they left me."

That was funny.

The next night I had courtside seats to the game. The Knicks tried to bump me at the last minute because they were saying they had too many requests from movie stars. I stood my ground. I'd gone to a preseason game and sat about 20 rows back while all the Yankees sat up front. Yeah, they were in the playoffs at the time, but they hadn't won the World Series yet. Of course, I hadn't won a damn thing, but **I wanted to be on the court.** The game's a lot different when you're sitting close. All those years I spent sneaking into the Laker games, sitting way up in the nosebleed section. One of the first things I did when I got my money was buy Lakers season tickets, right behind Jack Nicholson, on the floor at the Forum. I was not about to be **bumped** by **Robert De Niro** or **Joe Torre** or anybody at the Garden when my team, the Lakers, were in town.

During the game I saw a guy I'd met a few times sitting courtside. I knew him only as Wes. I was looking around, saw Michael J. Fox, Mariah Carey, and suddenly, there was Wes.

"Who is that guy?" I asked.

I'd seen him on TV holding Michael Irvin's helmet on the sidelines of the Cowboy games, I'd seen him on the sidelines at the Super Bowl in Tempe, Arizona. I'd seen him courtside at a bunch of NBA games, hanging out with Michael Jordan, Scottie Pippen, Charles Barkley, and now here he was sitting a few seats down from me.

"Damn, what does that guy do?" I asked somebody.

I found out later that he had played with Michael Irvin at the University of Miami when Jimmy Johnson was there and had gone on to help recruit kids for him. He also had sold shoes and suits along the way to players all over the NFL and the NBA. He was everywhere.

Wes got up and talked to Spike Lee, and then to the TNT folks at the game. I guess he's one of the guys you get around you when you're a pro athlete. Wes isn't an athlete anymore, but **Wes has serious juice.**

"Bet they didn't try bumping his ass for no movie star," I said.

The Lakers won. And when it was over, I talked for a minute with Cedric Ceballos and Eddie Jones and Kobe, of course. Some of the Knicks came by, too, all commenting on my attire for the evening—baggy jeans, boots, flannel shirt, a big down ski vest, and a beanie.

"Man, dog," one of them said, "you're scaring people off, looking like you're going to go shoot someone. You look like some **little thug** out of California."

I just laughed. I did look like a little thug out of California.

Styles in Los Angeles and New York are very different. Not just the clothing. The music's not as hard-core in New York, especially the rap. On the West Coast, we've always been on the cutting edge there. But the **clubs are wilder** in New York, I think. Especially the *freaks,* what old people call *groupies.* They've always come on to me a lot, but I've never seen such bold styles as what I've gotten from some women in New York. They say all kinds of **scary shit.**

"He is a beautiful *black* man," one of them said to a friend of mine, emphasizing black. "No, he's *the* beautiful *black* man. You tell him, I'd do anything to him if I was with him."

That shit makes me laugh.

A few months ago I went to the Official All Star Cafe in New York for a party thrown by Tyra Banks. She'd made some swimsuit calendar or something, and invited a bunch of so-called celebrities to help kick it off. Scottie Pippen was there with some of his boys and I went with a couple of my friends. The funny thing was, there were hardly any women there at all. I guess Tyra didn't want anyone *upstaging her.* After a minute, we all left and went somewhere else to get something to eat. Bold women, these New Yorkers.

By game time I was bored and ready to play. Practice was getting on my nerves. Yeah, we had a W, but we'd also just had a week where I'd relaxed and had a lot of fun, then had to come **back to the same bullshit.** Worst of all, the night before the game we—as usual—were locked up in a hotel with an 11 p.m. curfew and weak TV. It was killing me. I was with Alex Van Dyke, my on-the-road roommate, and we were watching *The Nutty Professor* while at the same time USC was battling hard against Stanford, and Mike Tyson was getting whupped by Evander Holyfield. I never sleep well the night before games, and now I was pissed because my school ended up losing and I missed one of the best fights in a long time. Next time, Tyson better fight in the off-season. I heard Magic was sitting ringside. Next time, I plan to be right there next to him.

Game day against New England was cold, but clear. We had a **21-point lead and lost** by four points, 31–27. They threw me the ball exactly one time in the first half, which was fine because we were moving the ball on the ground and we had a big lead. But when things started to go bad in the second half, the coaches froze.

It's the only thing they know how to do. We were up

over Miami 14–0, the Redskins 10–3, Jacksonville 14–3, and Buffalo 15–9—and lost them all. Every single one. I thought the Arizona game had given us a taste of what it's like to hold a lead in the fourth quarter and not cave in. Man, I was **wrong.**

We got **tricked** and **licked** by the Patriots—they ran a flea-flicker, a reverse, everything but the Statue of Liberty play. Bill Parcells threw it all at us. At halftime, the Patriots made adjustments. They started double-teaming Hugh Douglas, back for his first game after breaking his ankle. Hugh had been all over the place during the first half: two sacks and a fumble. We didn't do shit.

And, of course, we got robbed by the officials—again. The Patriots ended up scoring what would be the winning touchdown after the refs gave—*gave*—them a first down when it was very clear that Victor Green nailed Ben Coates a yard short on fourth down. The offense was already halfway across the field when we saw where the dude spotted the ball.

"He never went over the 50," Victor was screaming.

Bring back the instant replay. ***THAT SPOT* probably cost us the game.** Still, we shouldn't have been in that position, not when we led 21–0.

We had a shot to beat them in the last drive. Frank Reich was humming and moved us from our own 24-yard line to the Patriots' 11-yard line with 56 seconds to play. We had five wide receivers and four downs. I really thought we were going to win.

On first down, though, Frank had to throw it away. On second down he threw at Chrebet but Otis Smith, a guy we had cut before the season began, tipped it away. On third down, finally, Frank looked at me, but **launched it too high.** I saw it coming and knew there was no way I'd get to it, so I fell to the turf and started pointing at the defender, hoping the official would call interference and we'd get the first down from the one. Didn't happen.

On fourth down Frank looked for Jeff Graham, who was having a great game. Graham was there, but so was Lawyer Milloy, a big dude I had gotten to know pretty well from college. He had played for Washington and we'd had some big battles. He had knocked the shit out of me earlier in the game, and now he tipped the ball away from Jeff. *Patriots win.*

I was so pissed off I could hardly talk. I walked into the locker room, disgusted.

"It's not the players' fault," I started hollering at our assistant coaches. "We've got talent out there and we're playing hard every single down. It's y'all, y'all have no idea how to win."

Everyone just stared at me.

And then I left, having yet again to walk up the ramp from the stadium in front of all the players from the other team, a loser. **That walk kills me.**

"Hey, dog," I heard someone yell at me. It was another one of my buddies who played for the Patriots, Willie McGinest, who had played at USC.

"Just keep balling, just keep balling," he said, a big smile on his face. "You're representing, dog, you're representing."

I had to laugh. Big Willie still speaking L.A. street-lingo way across the country.

Lawyer came up, too. We had hung out a lot in L.A.

this past summer. My guys, Derek Hazely and Marlin Lewis, were trying to recruit him for one of my agents, Lee Kolligian, and Lawyer liked hanging out with us. He didn't sign with Lee, but the friendship had been struck.

"Damn, you got good," I said to him. **"You knocked me** $good$ on that one play across the middle."

Lawyer just laughed.

I went over and found Terry Glenn and congratulated him on a good game. Terry and I are cool. We hung out down in Florida in December 1995 when we were both up for the Fred Biletnikoff Award for college football's wide receiver of the year. Everybody I knew thought I'd win it, but when the winner was announced, it wasn't me, but Terry.

All week before the Patriots game, the media had been trying to make a big deal out of the matchup between me and Glenn.

"Hell, I don't play against him," I said. "He doesn't guard me and I don't guard him. How the hell can you compare us because of that?"

Plus, we ran four- and five-receiver sets. The Patriots ran with two. And they fed Terry Glenn. They got him the ball. **They didn't use him to clear people out.**

Bill Parcells got into the act, too, saying they wanted Glenn over me all along. But this was after Terry got out of Parcells's dog house. He was hurt in the preseason, with a pulled hamstring, prompting Parcells to call him "she." Now that he was balling, though, Terry Glenn was Parcells's boy.

"Keyshawn's not even the best receiver on the Jets'

squad," Parcells said. "Wayne Chrebet's getting all the third-down passes."

He was right about the second part. I know he was just trying to build up Glenn, but it still **pissed me off.**

Terry Glenn had six catches for 83 yards against us. I had four for 44 yards. He was on track to beat out everyone for NFL Rookie of the Year if he kept playing like he was and if they kept feeding him the ball. And he got this win.

Damn, I was pissed. I drove home and went to bed. I wasn't going out for a long, long time. No more. Hell, I was 1–9, people were going to be *laughing at me.* I planned on staying inside until next season.

The morning after the Patriots game I walked into camp and went straight upstairs to talk to Shack Harris. I was sitting in his office when Dick Haley came in, and then Kotite.

"Y'all pay me **too much money** to have me just **run up and down the field,**" I told them. "When we started losing, you needed to get me the ball. Just get me the ball and we'll win."

"You should have come to me and let me know you weren't getting it," Kotite said.

I had let him know during the Buffalo game and during the Arizona game, and he had gone straight to Erhardt and screamed at him to get me the ball.

"Next time, you just got to let me know," he said. "You gotta let me know what's happening."

A lot of people think the head coach ought to know

that on his own. But whether I was getting the ball or not really fell on Erhardt, who was supposed to make sure that that happened. He needed to go. We needed somebody who could run the offense and coach a damn football game.

Kotite had another problem on his mind. Frank Reich had been playing great football. But now, our $25 million man was getting ready to make a comeback after dislocating his shoulder. Old coaches always say a player doesn't lose his position because of an injury. I thought we ought to make an exception. Reich should stay in at quarterback. We had six games left—fuck it. Leave him in and let O'Donnell sit. They were paying me a hell of a lot of money for doing nothing, why not O'Donnell, too?

10

The ball was **there.** It was there, floating down into my hands in slow motion. We were behind by five points and down to the last play of the game. And the ball was there. It was one of those *surreal moments* I think I'll never, ever forget. Frank Reich was bleeding all over himself after getting whacked in the chin on the previous play. We had battled hard—I mean hard—all game long against the Indianapolis Colts. We were all beat up. My body was screaming at me.

"C'mon, Frank, **find me,** baby," I yelled over at Reich as we ran to the line.

Frank wiped the blood onto his pants and got ready to take the snap. Dude was glassy-eyed. I don't think he was all there but damn if he didn't launch a perfect Hail Mary to the right side of the end zone. If I couldn't get it, I was supposed to try to tip it to someone on our team. But it had my name all over it. I was there just waiting, watching, positioning myself to pull it in.

Unfortunately, I'd drawn a crowd. All around me were about six Colts, who were desperately trying not to get burned. Still, I had a good four inches on all of them. I leaped high in the air, reaching up as far as I could. I touched it, I felt it. The ball was in my hands, leather against skin. I tried to squeeze it tight, pull it in, **win the game, be a hero,** be what I was dying to be ever since I started playing ball. Right then, though, the Colts' defenders jumped on me, knocking my feet up in the air just as I was trying to pull the ball in. I watched it skitter away. **No** play. **No** touchdown. **Nothing.** I never had possession. The game was over and we lost, again, by less than a touchdown to a team, like a bunch of others, we could have, should have beaten.

I lay on the ground in **agony** for a few minutes. Not making that catch, not being able to be the man who would win the game, the hero, and losing it to go 1–10 on the season, it hurt like hell.

"Key, Key, man, it's O.K.," Jeff Graham said to me as I got up to run off the field.

I shoved him away.

My old high school teammate, Lamont Warren, a running back with the Colts, came over to try to console me, too. Well, I don't know how bad he felt; he won the damn game.

"Hey, Key," Lamont was saying, trying to put his arm around me.

I shrugged him off, too. My misery didn't need any company. We had now **lost 10 games**—into double digits in the loss column. I felt **deflated,** all the sizzle drained out of my body. So much emotion skittered away with that ball onto the turf. Damn, I didn't want this to happen to me, I thought.

Nobody could believe what had happened.

"Maybe we're living on an Indian burial ground," defensive tackle Hugh Douglas said.

We had led for much of the game, but couldn't get the

W even though we had a last drive that was as good as any we'd had all year. Everybody was really down. Especially Kotite. He looked **suicidal,** and when he told us to take Monday and Tuesday off, the thought crossed my mind that he was headed for the cliffs and we'd never see him again.

"Everybody needs a break," he said, announcing his decision. "You played hard, take a break. Get away from all this. See you Wednesday."

To me, that meant getting my butt to Los Angeles. The team flew back to New York, and then first thing Monday morning, Jeff Graham and I took off for the sunshine. I needed to *get far, far away from this MESS,* back to something familiar, back to something positive, back to where I wasn't a player on a 1-and-10 team. Jeff, who had a wonderful game—three touchdowns and 189 yards receiving—decided he'd like to see all that, too, find out what my world in L.A. was like. We decided on the plane **not even to think about the Jets** until we got back. It was that, or go fucking mad.

So we did L.A. I took him everywhere. And I mean everywhere. From Beverly Hills to the 'hood and back. We hit a few clubs, went and saw a bunch of the guys I used to hang with in the old days, played with my baby, and drove out to the Valley, where my mom's house was getting built. We had to make sure the Jacuzzi was being put in just right.

"Mile a minute," Jeff told a friend of mine when we got back. "Here, there, here, there, buzz, buzz, buzz. Never stopped moving, not once."

That was true. And all it did was make me want to get

home for good even more. ***Five more games,*** I kept telling myself. Five more games and I'm back on my home turf, where life was sane.

Jeff and I took a red-eye back Tuesday night, landing just in time to change clothes and head to practice. I was tired as hell. I also realized I really didn't care as much anymore about trying to do something this season. ***This season was over.*** There was **no hope** of doing anything now. Strangely, the beat writers for the team sensed that something had changed in me. They wanted to know where my energy was, how I was feeling, what did the loss to the Colts do to me? They knew something had happened inside of me when we lost that damned game, although honestly I was mainly just beat from taking that red-eye back and going right in to practice.

But those reporters were funny. They were soft-spoken and timid, like I was some mental case. And none of them knew I'd gone to L.A., which cheered me up immensely. Fooling reporters. I love that, especially this crew.

I walked into WNBC Wednesday night to tape my weekly show with Len Berman.

"So is Kotite going to make it through the season?" he asked while he was getting his makeup put on.

"Didn't you hear?" I said, sounding all concerned.

"Hear what?"

"The Jets have called a press conference for 11 o'clock tomorrow morning. We have a team meeting right before."

"Is he gone, is he gone?" Berman asked, jumping up from his chair. "How are we going to deal with this, our show doesn't air until Saturday? How do we handle this? What are we doing to do?"

"Aw, I'm just messing with you," I said. He didn't laugh.

Earlier in the night I had said the same thing to Kelly Neal, a producer from ESPN who broke the story of me reaching terms with the team way back in August. I had her going for a minute, too. **The media.** *They make me laugh.*

Everyone told me I had to be careful in New York.

"They'll eat you up," someone said.

But I really haven't had any problems. Why? Because I don't care what they write. I really don't. Yeah, one of the first things I did every day was get one of those packets that the PR staff put together of all the stories written about the Jets. I liked seeing what kind of crazy shit they all wrote. They're all nosy as hell. Especially Rich Cimini from the New York *Daily News*. That guy's **nosy** and **obnoxious.** My buddy Skeats came in on Monday after the Colts game. Skeats had just finished up his last season at Portland State and flew out to spend some time with me in New York. Skeats can ball, I'll tell you that. I'm going to get him some sort of tryout with the Jets sometime soon. **Hell, just about ANYONE can play on a 1–10 team.**

"Put some pads on and get out here," Jeff Graham yelled at Skeats when he was at practice on Wednesday. Skeats just laughed.

"Hey, Wes," I called out, talking about that dude, Wes, who's always on the sidelines holding Michael Irvin's helmet. We had seen him during the Cowboys–Packers game on Monday night.

"If you ain't gonna play," I said, "you just be Wes."

Cimini caught wind of our conversation and found out who Skeats was and how we'd been friends since junior high school. So he tried to interview Skeats, who is 6' 3", 220 pounds, and not much of a conversationalist.

"Can I ask you a couple of questions?" he asked Skeats.

"What are the questions?" Skeats asked back.

"Well, you know, how Keyshawn's dealing with the season, all the losses, what he thinks of New York," Cimini said.

"You'll have to ask him," said Skeats.

Nobody asked Skeats any more questions.

I'd been living the entire season at the Marriott Residence Inn in Plainview, Long Island, *even though I told everybody I had moved to Long Beach.* I had a two-bedroom suite with three TVs and a VCR and room service. I didn't need anything else this year, I thought. I was building a million-dollar house in the Valley and renting another apartment for Shikiri and the baby in Westwood, so I didn't need to buy more furniture and bother with getting another place set up. I'd worry about all that next season.

But when the media got wise to where I was staying, they started calling the front desk asking for me. I told the staff to tell anybody who asked that I had moved, and I changed my name on the register to Frank White—the name, it just so happens, of the main character in a Laurence Fishburne movie, *King of New York*.

I thought I'd be king by now, but ***nobody's king when you're 1–10.***

Except for Cimini, the team's beat writers are basically O.K. Gerry Eskenazi from *The New York Times*, the veteran of the reporter pack, is **pretty cool.** He's always trying to find out something that the others don't know—they're all doing that in one way or another—but Gerry's cool. He writes it straight without any kind of wild slant to it. And he's got a headline writer who doesn't need to write some sensationalistic shit just to sell newspapers.

All the guys from *The New York Times* are pretty classy: Eskenazi, George Vecsey, and Bill Rhoden. But Dave Hutchinson from The Newark *Star-Ledger* is *sneaky.* Dude looks just like Sammy Davis Jr., and he's always leaning in trying to hear other people's conversations. We're just careful not to say much when he's doing that. Mark Cannizzaro from the *New York Post* is kind of sneaky, too. I like Steve Serby from the *New York Post* and Randy Lange from The Bergen County *Record*.

The guys from WFAN had been pretty good to me since they ripped me at the beginning of the season. I went on the air with them a couple of times. I guess everybody else from the Jets was too scared.

It was the TV guys who really made me laugh, mainly because they had ***no clue about what was going on.*** At least the beat reporters were there every day, looking to stir up shit. The TV guys would show up for about four minutes of practice, make some ridiculous assessment of the team, do a stand-up with practice going on behind them, then book.

On the national front I like Ahmad Rashad and Bob Costas from NBC, and Dan Patrick from ESPN. Patrick's **funny as hell.** I even like Joe Theismann. He came out and did an interview with me after he made his "jerk" statements. That was **pretty stand-up.** I like Sterling Sharpe, too. People laugh at this, but I also really like Dr. Jerry Punch and Adrian Carsten from ESPN. When I was playing high school ball, those guys were the sideline reporters for college football. Still are, I think. We'd pretend to be them and start interviewing each other after the games. I still haven't met Dr. Punch. I met Lee Corso and Craig James when we played Notre Dame my senior year. They were cool. But they ain't Dr. Punch.

Every day, either before or after practice, depending on the schedule, the group of beat writers and assorted TV and radio guys would position themselves right at my locker, which was in the corner of the locker room, I guess because it had the most space. In 1995, they crowded around Boomer Esiason, who would tell them all kinds of politically correct stories. When the $25 million man took Boomer's place, and was pretty much of a **bore,** they were starving for someone to give them good stuff to write. I've never seen a group of reporters so happy to see me as they were when I arrived at camp on August 5. *I was their quote savior.*

Wayne Chrebet's locker was to my right and Jeff Graham's was to the left. It wasn't unusual to see both of those guys totally ignored by the media horde. I learned that if the locker room was open to reporters from 10:30 a.m. to 11:15 a.m., I should show up at about 11:05, which I suppose was why they stood around my little cubicle: They didn't want to miss anything. Their questions were sometimes okay, sometimes stupid, but I was pretty careful to say the right stuff. A couple of times I'd gone off—like when I said I should be starting—but I'd always been me, which I think they all appreciated.

"Imagine if this team didn't have me," I told one of them one day late in the season. *"You fools would have nothing, **nothing** to be putting in all those newspaper stories. Y'all should be thankful I'm around and still happy and talking to y'all."*

But I wasn't happy. I was miserable. Losing like that just ate at me. We weren't going anywhere and that was depressing. Every day I woke up thinking, shit, we're 1–10. Fortunately, there were 50 other guys who were 1–10, too. We were all sorry, but we were sorry together.

Jeff Graham and I had gotten real tight. After we both hurt our knees we hung out a lot at my place, both our legs propped up on the coffee table, packed in ice. His parents came to all the games and sometimes spent the week at his house. His mother is a **great cook** and I would fly down the highway to his place anytime I heard that it was her night in the kitchen.

Other guys were cool, too. Victor Green, Aaron Glenn, and I went at each other hard every day in practice, but we laughed when the play was over, calling each other dog this, dog that. This was a cool group of guys with a lot of talent, and the thing I liked best was that while I knew we were out of it, *nobody—nobody—was giving up,* refusing to play hard. Well, there were some dudes just happy to be collecting their paychecks, guys who could not have cared less if we ever won another game. But hell, ***they'll be gone anyway,*** sooner or later. After the Colts loss I thought about giving up, but I've got too much pride.

Someone asked me around this time whether, right then, I would take less money to play for a winning team. I thought for a minute and said no. Not because of the money—I would make money wherever I went—but because **I do believe in this team.** We've got to have changes—Erhardt, at least, has to go. If that happens, I swear we'll win games in 1997. We'll be in the playoffs then, or at least by '98. I hate losing more than about anything in the world. But hell ... I'm here. I remember the first time we played Indianapolis, and Lamont Warren and I were on the field before the game. We looked at each other and just started laughing. We had been through so much together and overcome so much shit. And here we were, together on an NFL field on a Sunday afternoon.

"Hey, dog," he said. "We're in the league. We're in the league."

"Yeah, dog," I answered. **"We here."**

A few nights after the second Colts game, I went into Manhattan to receive an award from the Starlight Foundation for my charity work with children. It was a big, fancy party, with two huge bars set up and basically no food in sight. No black people in sight, either, except for me, Tamecus, and Skeats.

"Lot of Republicans here," I said, looking around.

I signed a bunch of autographs and posed for pictures. The place was **mobbed.** Then it came time for me to accept my award and help auction off a mini-helmet I had signed. With it came a trip to Jets training camp next summer. The bids got pretty high, with $1,500 going once, going twice before I cut in.

"Add two tickets to any game to the pot," I whispered to the auctioneer.

"Keyshawn Johnson has just added two tickets to any Jets game next season, courtesy of No. 19," the guy said. The crowd roared and we got the price up to $1,700. That made me feel good. Michael Jordan's autographed jersey went for $4,100. That was okay. *In a few years, mine will go for* **double** *that.* And not just because of inflation.

On the Thursday after the Colts game, I found out that tight end Johnny Mitchell, who had played college ball at Nebraska and spent four years with the Jets and two weeks with the Dolphins before going a little wacko and retiring at age 25, had signed with the Dallas Cowboys. That was pretty amazing. *Maybe I should go* ***wacko*** *and retire, too.*

They tell a story around Jets camp about Mitchell that I heard when I first got here. Seems Mitchell was a bit of an eccentric, to say the least. The team was practicing on the Astroturf field that abuts the players' parking lot. Somebody kicked the ball wide of the goal post (typical Jets' kicker) and the ball sailed way into the area where all the cars were parked like sitting ducks.

"Hey, the ball just hit a red Porsche," somebody yelled as a joke.

"What the hell?" Mitchell said as he was running onto the field for the next series.

Turned out Mr. Mitchell owned a red Porsche. He broke huddle and started sprinting to the parking lot to see if his car was O.K. **What team dedication.**

And now he's with the Cowboys. I know I said I'm happy playing for the Jets based on the future, but right now, man, *I'd love to be balling with the 'Boys.*

Let me be the clear-out man for Michael Irvin. I'd take the No. 2 spot, no problem. He'd be retiring right when I'd reach my prime. I'd say, let me in there, baby. I'd love to be playing for Barry Switzer. That's a man who can coach—he knows how to win and how to let players play!

BILLS 35 .... Jets 10

11

I never thought the season would be like this. I never thought I'd end up hating our coaches. I never thought I'd have to scream to get the ball thrown my way. **The season was *a mess*.** I was embarrassed, sick, disgusted, pissed as hell. This wasn't the way it was supposed to be. I really think the loss to Indianapolis, me not pulling that last Hail Mary pass in for six, killed us. I know it sucked the life right out of me.

The next week I had three drops against the Bills up in Buffalo. **Three big, fat, horrible drops.** Two were my fault. One was a toss-up. But damn, three drops?? I was supposed to have a big game—I tore them up last time at our place when we almost beat them. Three drops. Hell, I don't think I had three drops my entire senior season at USC.

I didn't get the job done. Period. Maybe the Jets were finally getting to me. Maybe this negative shit had finally seeped into my body.

But, damn. I dropped three balls and **_I sucked._** This time, **really sucked.** After the game, I was embarrassed, humiliated, and sick. And damn, my body hurt.

I flew back with the team and all I wanted to do was go home and crawl in bed and sleep for a hundred years—or at least through the four weeks left in the NFL season. But I had already bought **four courtside seats** to the Sonics–Knicks game that night at $1,000 a pop. And I wasn't about to waste $4,000 because I was embarrassed. So Skeats and Tamecus met Jeff Graham and me at the airport, and we drove into the city to see the game.

The Sonics killed the Knicks. Patrick Ewing went 2-for-15. Hell, I could have gone 2-for-15 from my seat. The TV cameras caught Jeff and me, and some ridiculous guy came up and asked me whether I could take Gary Payton or Shawn Kemp.

"Man, I got enough problems of my own right now without thinking about any of that," I said.

People around me laughed.

I tried to be myself, but damn if I didn't feel terrible about what had happened against Buffalo. We stood around talking with the Sonics after the game, and by the time we got to dinner on the Upper East Side I was starving. I ordered a salad, steak, shrimp, clam chowder—a ton of food. But when it came I realized *I was too messed up to even eat.* My hip was killing me, my shoulder felt like it had popped out of its socket, and my head was pounding.

"Just wrap all this up," I told the waiter. "I'm going to the car."

And I did. I left Jeff, Skeats, and Tamecus at the table and I went outside to my Jeep, let the seat back, and *went to sleep,* *right there on the street.* It had been a terrible, terrible day.

I didn't feel much better the next day when I woke up, either. I was hearing from back home that John Robinson's job was in jeopardy because USC had lost to UCLA—again—and they had to play Notre Dame next. *There was NO WAY IN HELL John Robinson deserved to lose that job.* The problem wasn't John Robinson. He's a coach you want to play for and play hard for. He's a player's guy and I know dozens of athletes who came to USC just because he was there. I honestly believe he's the best thing to happen to that football program and to the inner city of Los Angeles in a long, long time. He does a lot of great things around there that people don't know about. And by people, I mean the USC athletic director, Mike Garrett, who has torn down some good people and some good programs because he's obsessed with power. *He's a little dude with a Napoleon complex*—thinks he's got to one-up everyone or else he won't get the respect he thinks he deserves. That man has none of my respect. Ever since he fired Charlie Parker, the basketball coach, in the middle of last season, I've had **nothing** to do with the man. Garrett thinks he's smarter than any coach and believes he needs to be in on every coaching decision. Hell, he ran George Raveling off, and then tried to tell Parker what kind of offense he should run and why certain players should play ahead of others.

He's tried to run the football team for J-Rob, too, but Robinson wouldn't stand for it. Frankly, J-Rob's got more juice at that school than Garrett, and I think Garrett needs to be thinking real hard about what he'll be taking on if he fires Robinson, or anyone on his staff for that matter. The alumni are critical, that's true. We went 9-2-1 my senior season and the losses were to UCLA and

Notre Dame. I swear people came up to me and said they'd rather go 2–9 with the only wins coming over those two schools. So it's a **tough** group, but Robinson is a **damned good** coach and people should realize that. Hell, we beat the new genius, Gary Barnett, and Northwestern in the Rose Bowl my senior year. I guess that doesn't carry very far into the next season.

John Robinson taught me so much about the game of football and about life. He gave me a lot. If it wasn't for him when I was a little kid, hanging out on the field, I doubt I would have ended up playing football at all. For sure not at USC. When he came back, that's where I wanted to go. And he hadn't forgotten me, either. Once I got my act together at West L.A., he was calling. A lot. People didn't believe that *he'd call me just about every night,* checking in on me, seeing how I was doing in school and practice.

Because of all the trouble I'd caused Mississippi State and the fact that I probably could have caused just as much trouble for Cal or Texas Tech (the other schools I visited), a lot of schools stopped recruiting me. Nobody wanted to mess with a player **with my kind of baggage** —a scam artist, a kid who wouldn't work hard. I was a troublemaker, they thought, an angry street kid with no discipline and no heart.

Nobody knew that getting shot had changed me, a lot. I also had eventually realized that I wasn't going to be able to scam my way into school, that I had to do the work. And so I did. But nobody knew that. **I was still**

this messed-up little STREET RAT with no future. Arizona dropped me, Cal dropped me. Nobody, it seemed, was interested. ***Nobody except Coach Robinson*** was willing to spend the time to see that I had changed, that I had grown up.

I spent a lot of time the spring before my second year at West L.A. hanging out on the USC practice field—just like when I was a little kid. Only this time I wasn't stealing ROTC backpacks and bicycles. This time I was trying to learn. I talked with a lot of the assistant coaches, none of whom knew much about me. They said they'd heard of me, but nothing more than that I was a great high school player.

"Hey, just **remember my name,**" I said.

I actually had enough credits that spring to get my degree, but I knew I needed a solid season on the football field to attract anyone's attention. Robinson had everybody at USC keeping tabs on me, checking all my transcripts—by then I had credits from three different junior colleges—and had all kinds of compliance counselors calling. They found out that I'd worked hard. After my first game that fall, Robinson was on the phone that night offering me a scholarship. I'd start school there in January.

"Finally," I said when I called my mother to tell her the news. "I'm in. It's going to happen, mom. I'm going to play for USC and I'm going to the league. ***It's all going to happen,*** just like we planned."

I did enroll in January and went through spring drills and the spring game. It was pretty evident that not only was I going to start in the fall, but I also was going to be the **go-to guy.** But I wasn't really prepared physically when I got to camp. Two-a-days burned up my thighs so bad that I could hardly walk. I was taking a beating emotionally, too, when *The Los Angeles Times* reported that there was **a warrant out for my arrest** in connection with a stolen pager and cell phone. They wrote that the police report said it was me, but pointed out that my birth date was a year and a month off.

I never stole any of that shit. If I had, I wouldn't have gotten caught, that's for sure. To this day I don't know what happened. Somebody was saying he was me and the police bought the act. But all this had hit the papers and I was upset and pissed off. I went to the police and turned myself in, told them what I knew, and they scheduled a court date. But when it came time for me to get my day, they couldn't find any of the victims or the witnesses. **Case dropped.** I stayed pissed off at the *L.A. Times* all season.

My legs were still in bad shape when the season began. So bad that they wouldn't let me play at all against Penn State the second game of the season. In our first game, against Washington at home, I had caught only one pass, for five yards.

That game was wild for me. It was the first game of the season and the very first time I'd run out of the tunnel onto the field at the Los Angeles Coliseum, where I'd sat in the stands and watched USC play a hundred times. *I cried.* **For real.** I realized all I'd worked for and dreamed about had come true. Looking back, I'd have to say that it was an overwhelming feeling. It was a big step for me, towards my future; none of that was lost on me as I ran with the team to the sidelines.

When I caught that first pass, though, it was something else. Rob Johnson threw the ball so hard and I wanted to catch it so bad that I just sort of collided with the ball. The impact of the hit **knocked my helmet clean off.** At a football camp in the summer of '96 some little kid asked me what my most embarrassing moment had been—that was it.

The third game of the season, though, I had four catches for 105 yards against Baylor and never looked back. I'd go on a 12-game streak (leading into my senior year) of catching balls for more than 100 yards. We beat Cal that year 61–0, letting me get back at one of the schools that had dropped me—and then some. I got a little excited on the field after I made a catch and started taunting the DB, which got me a 15-yard penalty and benched for the next series. I figured out I had to *tone things down a little bit,* but I still managed to be me.

We also beat up on Arizona, another school that had dropped me. I had five catches for 109 yards and publicly declared that "Desert Swarm"—the so-called tough-as-hell Arizona defense—was dead.

That season I ended up with 66 catches for 1,362 yards and nine touchdowns, and I started wondering whether I should turn pro then, rather than spend the next season worrying about staying eligible in school and off the operating table. In the Cotton Bowl, I only confused myself more by having the biggest game of my career—eight catches for a *Cotton Bowl–record 222 yards* and three touchdowns. We beat up on Texas Tech, another school that had dropped me, 55–14.

I spent an **agonizing week** after the bowl game trying to decide what to do. If I left school, I'd be a first-rounder, probably in the top 20 somewhere, and an instant millionaire. If I stayed, I could finish school, which was important to my mother, and have a chance at the Heisman and all the honors that would come with a great senior season. I talked with a lot of people—Bobby Beathard from the San Diego Chargers, Jeff Fisher in Houston, Shack Harris of the Jets—teachers, friends, old coaches. In the end, I decided to stay. The real reason wasn't the Heisman or the glory or the hype—all that was cool—but the real reason I stayed was because **I loved college football**—I always have—and I wanted one more year to leave my mark.

The summer before my senior season I worked out with a couple of teammates and the USC strength coach, James Strom. Damn, and I thought I knew about working out. He had us running in the sand dunes, starting with six reps up and down, finally getting to 12 reps up and down. It was miserable, exhausting. I couldn't even keep food down at first. Dude was killing me. I was dizzy, sick, totally spent by the end of the day. But it worked—I came into camp with a lot more muscle mass and about 10 more pounds. My body has always responded well to weight training and all that, but, man, I was cut and ready.

Earlier in the spring, *Sports Illustrated* had called to tell me they were planning to put me on the cover and pick us to win the national championship. I thought they were playing with me at first, but the more I thought about it, the more I realized that we had a hell of a team and yeah, maybe we could bring the national trophy home. I think that's what made me endure those killer workouts, I really thought it could all be ours.

And then came the derailing process. Once you're up and strong, there is always something—I don't care who or what you are—that will **try to bring you down.** It happens to black people every day in this society. And suddenly it was happening to me and to our football team, and **it came in the form of the NCAA.**

It all happened in early August, just as we were starting fall practice. The Pacific-10 Conference called the school and told them I'd been linked with an agent in San Diego, Elliott Vallin. They said that the NCAA had tapes of a conversation between Vallin and a guy who worked as a recruiter for several agents, Jesse Martinez, in which **Vallin *claims he gave me $1,200*** when I was at West L.A. The *Houston Chronicle* reported all this and it spread like wildfire through not only Southern California, but across the country. *Sports Illustrated* called and got ready to rewrite their entire story, yank me off the cover, and drop us from a predicted first-place finish to somewhere in the bottom half of the Top 10—that's how **freaked** people were.

Mike Garrett called me into his office and told me what was going on. Before I knew it, I was talking with a Pac-10 investigator about my relationship with Elliott Vallin and Jesse Martinez. It was all a bunch of lies and to this day if I ever see Jesse Martinez, his face is going to meet up with my fists. He was trying to claim some ink for himself as this do-good, tell-all guy. He'd become a so-called informant to the NCAA the year before, giving them the information that Joey Galloway, a football player at Ohio State, took $200 from an agent in Chicago. Galloway was suspended for two games. Martinez also told the NCAA that Arizona basketball player Damon Stoudamire's father got a plane ticket from Steve Feldman, an agent in Newport Beach. Stoudamire was booted out of Arizona's last regular-season game, although he was allowed to play in the national tournament after the NCAA found out he had done nothing wrong.

Now Martinez was trying to get me, and he nearly ruined my season. I do blame him for ruining Skeats's season at Iowa.

What happened was this: Elliott Vallin used to be partners with Tim Shannon—the guy who took me in when I was a ball boy at USC. He's a guy I've known most of my life and a guy I consider as near a part of my family as anyone. When my roommate at West L.A. moved out, a month before Karim Abdul Jabbar moved in, I was strapped for money. I couldn't afford that month's rent, so I called Tim Shannon and **asked to borrow $200— period.** No $1,200 to $15,000 as some people were saying. A mere $200. And he cut me a check. That was it.

The NCAA *eventually cleared me,* but then they started investigating Skeats. They talked to everybody in my family, everybody in Skeats's family, and wouldn't let the issue die. They found out that we had gone to lunch and a Dodger game with Tim and Elliott, and were messing with us about another $200 check that was sent to

Skeats's house. I didn't know who it was from or what it was for. The check was from somebody in San Diego and Skeats's mom thought it was for one of her daughters, who did a lot of modeling down there. I think now it was from someone trying to get to me through Skeats's mom. I had stayed there for a while and people knew we all needed the money. To this day, though, I still don't know everything that went on or why.

The one thing that both John Robinson and, surprisingly, Mike Garrett did was stick by me. I told them both straight out that I didn't take anything from anybody illegally. I had a lot of family and friends around and when I needed money, I asked them. I considered Tim Shannon in that group. Basically Robinson told the NCAA to stick it. I was more clear—I told them in several heated meetings to **go _fuck_ themselves,** that they had nothing on me, and if they tried suspending me—even tried—I'd be taking their asses to court. I stormed out of a lot of those meetings, leaving the investigators with their mouths hanging open. All they were trying to do was bring me down, bring USC down.

The University of Iowa didn't stand by Skeats, though. He hadn't played a down for them yet—he redshirted his first year there even though they had promised him he wouldn't have to redshirt. When the NCAA shit started, they just ran the other way. I guess he wasn't the franchise player I was. They held him out two games and made him donate the value of the lunch and the Dodgers ticket to a charity. I think it came to something like $29.32. Just for having lunch with me and my friends when we were starving in junior college. **Tell me**

that's fair. Tell me anything about the NCAA is
fair. We were starving, but we were making millions of
dollars for institutions that pay inept administrators hundreds of thousands of dollars a year in salaries. ***We
starve while they get fat.***

What beat Skeats down was that by the time Iowa decided they didn't have to be chicken anymore and lifted
the suspension on him, their starters were set. He barely
got in a game the rest of the season. His grades dropped
and he came real close to quitting, walking away from the
whole mess. He talked a lot about coming home, getting
a 9-to-5. Instead, he decided to transfer to Portland State
to finish up. It wasn't right. I hold the NCAA directly re-
sponsible for all of Skeats's problems at Iowa. He could
have been a starter, made it to the league the same time
as me. But the ***NCAA started in on him and
Iowa wilted.***

Nobody could believe I told the Pac-10 and the NCAA
to go to hell. They never did anything to me, although I
know some of my teammates paid the price. Shawn Wal-
ters and Israel Ifeanyi both were suspended because of
contact with agents. Shawn's stuff was a lot more serious
than Izzy's. Everyone was saying they took Izzy because
they couldn't get me. Probably true.

One thing I was not about to do was let all this stuff with
the NCAA mess with my head. I had given up too much
to play a final season at USC, and I wasn't going mental
now. Even with all that stuff going on, I had a wonderful
season. Yeah, we lost to Notre Dame and then to

UCLA—both losses just about killed me—but we had some great moments along the way.

Our game against Stanford was a **ball-buster.** We went down to the wire. We win, we had a shot at the Rose Bowl. We lose and who knows what happens. I caught the winning touchdown to make it 31–30, and then Robinson put me back in on defense and I ended up breaking up a Stanford pass that would have given them a chance to kick a winning field goal. That victory was as good as I've ever felt about football. We *won* and we were going to the ***Rose Bowl.*** That was *sweet.*

The month before the Rose Bowl I was supposed to have my knee 'scoped (the same knee that I did have 'scoped earlier this season). But I worked hard rehabbing and stayed off it for a while, and in the end, decided to just play on it and see what happened.

What happened was a glorious game and a perfect end to my college career. All the hype building up to the game was on Northwestern and their miracle season. That was just fine with me. I was happy they had all the attention. Reporters jump on anybody's bandwagon and they decided to spend all their time talking to those little munchkin DBs who claimed they were going to be able to stop me.

Our practices were pretty quiet, media-wise. But we were burning up the field all week long. Things were really working for us and we were all ready to show the country how good we were, even if we weren't going to win the national title. That week, J-Rob put in a bunch of plays for me, which was cool. **I was even going to throw a pass**—a touchdown route back to Rob Johnson. That was until Mark Schwarz of ESPN went on the air and told the world we had been working on it in practice that day. That was the end of my pass-throwing career and the end of Schwarz's access to our locker room. Damn, the coaches were pissed at him. I was too. I could have been the only player in Rose Bowl history to catch a TD and throw for one, too.

I was still pissed off at the USC student paper, too. They'd been down on us all season, picking us to lose this game or that game. They were our own student paper and they were saying all this shit? I stopped talking to the little dudes who wrote for them and I got a lot of other guys to stop, too. I guess it was cool, to them, to rip us. Just like it was cool for the reporters to be in Northwestern's cheering section—but only until the game started. Then it was time to cheer for me—*I ended up with 12 catches for 216 yards* (a Rose Bowl record), one touchdown, and the **Rose Bowl MVP trophy.**

And that ended Northwestern's miracle season.

12

By now I'd figured out that *the Jets lose* and that the only really interesting part of our games was *how* we lose. The Oilers game was another disaster. I knew it would be from the first minute. It was supposed to be the $25 million man's big comeback. All week long he'd been taking snaps with the first team in practice, still throwing little weak-ass two-yard routes to Chrebet, and now he was coming back as our fearless leader. And then—and this I'll never get over—he pulled a calf muscle in warmups. *He pulled a calf muscle in warmups.*

I wanted to see the calf. For real. How in the hell do you pull a calf muscle tossing a football around? *Half of me* says the dude was faking it so that Erhardt and Kotite could keep their jobs. It gave them a big, fat excuse as to why we were terrible. They could say, "Hey, we haven't had the $25 million man, how were we supposed to win?" O'Donnell was their boy and I think he went down maybe not to save Kotite, but definitely to save his guru, old-man Erhardt.

It didn't matter. We lost without him, but I bet we would have lost with him, too.

For me, it was another shitty game. So bad the fans started booing me. I can't blame them.

I knew it would happen sometime. I knew I'd drop one or two here and there, and I figured I'd hear the

195

boos—that's cool—but not during a game played in the middle of **a damned typhoon.** The rain was **pounding down** on us and the wind was **swirling.**

A lot of people had drops during the game. Mine just were highlighted a little more because I'd been talking all week—again—about them not getting me the ball. I told the coaches and any reporter around that I needed to get the ball early in the game, get involved, get my rhythm going.

There is nothing worse, to me, than dropping the damn football. It's there, you're open, you see it, you've got it, then *boom*—it's hitting the ground. Every day in practice I concentrate. I watch, I reach, I grab, and I bust my ass to catch that thing, even a meaningless little practice pass. I do it because you play how you practice. And I practice hard. Damned hard. But I'm **human.** I make ***mistakes.*** I've said before that I'm not a savior and I'm not superhuman. I have bad days. I snap at people. I forget to do things. Now, I'd dropped a couple of passes in a game. That hurt me. This had to stop. People were reminding me that Jerry Rice had an awful rookie year, and look at him now. I didn't feel like anything close to Jerry Rice, but that would change. I knew me.

But against Houston, they threw me the ball, I dropped it, and I got booed. At least by the fans who were there. We had **55,985 *no-shows.*** I caught a touchdown pass and actually finished up having a pretty decent game, but still, the whole day was a mess.

Houston played us pretty tough. Eddie George can ball, for real. Eddie George gets the ball. That's the biggest difference between us. Jeff Fisher, the coach at Houston, knows who to give the ball to to get the job done. I've known Fisher for a long time—since he played at USC and I was a ball boy. Fish came home one afternoon and I was in his apartment, raiding his refrigerator. I'd tagged along with his roommate and I was hungry. From then on, we became friends. I've talked with him a lot over the past couple of years. ***He's always been a guy who's given me advice straight.*** I'm happy for him, being down there with the Oilers. We talked for a minute before the game. I told him, like I tell any coach from any team I'd want to be playing for: "Save my career, get me out of here."

They just laugh. They know and I know that next year's going to be a whole lot different than this one was. But only if management does **the right thing.**

Reich had a ***horrible*** game. Probably because he didn't take any snaps—not one—with the first team all week. No surprise that he was off. We all had terrible games.

But the boos, damn, I hated hearing that. I was playing as hard as I could and yeah, I probably should have caught a few of those wet, soggy passes. But I didn't. ***Case closed. Game over. SEASON OVER.***

They threw beer on Kotite, too. I don't care who you are or what kind of coach you are, you ***don't deserve that.***

The week before the Houston game, I was home one night flipping channels on the tube when I came across something pretty amazing. It was the first airing of a documentary about two high school basketball teams from South Central Los Angeles—Crenshaw and Freemont. It was called *L.A. Champions* and was produced by a guy named Bob Drew, who has won a bunch of awards for documentaries he's done on everyone and everything from Gandhi to John F. Kennedy.

But to me the wildest thing about it was that Skeats and I had worked as security guards for the camera crews that filmed the games and the scenes all around the neighborhoods where we grew up. It was 1993 and we got paid $50 a day, which to us was ***pretty good money for doing nothing but having some fun,*** going to games for free, and acting like big shots because we were with all these TV people. We got these jobs because of Shelley Smith, whom we'd met a year earlier when we were doing nothing but getting into trouble and trying to figure out what to do with our lives.

Shelley, who helped me write this book, was writing an article for *Sports Illustrated* on the football team at Dorsey High School. We were gone from there and getting ready to head down to South Carolina to go to junior college. But we didn't want to **miss out on a chance to GET MENTIONED** in the article, so we started hanging out with her when she showed up each day to watch practice. We told her a lot of stories: Skeats punching the athletic director, how we looted stuff during the riots, how great we had been in high school, how we got robbed of a city championship against Banning. We hadn't met a lot of **white ladies from the suburbs** and she hadn't met many black kids from the inner city. It was cool.

We called her a couple of times when we were down south, asking how the article was coming, whether we'd be in it. And we called her when we came back, too. Mainly we wanted to know if she could help get us some work so that we could make some money on the side. And that's how we started with the documentary.

At first we worked a lot with a photographer named Dasal Banks, a big, black dude with a shaved head and an earring. He was cool. We took him all over the neighborhood, showing him the sights. And we worked the games, too, which was really cool because all our friends were there anyway—and we were getting paid.

Watching the documentary on TV really took me back. Things were so different then, and that was just three years ago. **Life was pretty lean** during those days. *We didn't have much to eat.* When Christmas came around, we didn't have money to buy anybody anything. It was tempting, at times, to go back to stealing from stores. I wanted to be the guy who would come home with armfuls of gifts for my mother and my brothers and sisters. But I had gotten myself back on track, trying to get to where I am now. So I just stayed **poor.**

Sometimes change is fast. Very fast.

The documentary turned out cool. I liked seeing something we had worked on end up on TV. The only thing I didn't like, though, was that Skeats and I didn't get into the credits; Shelley did, but they left us off. I wonder if any of the filmmakers realize now that I was the security kid, working for $50 a day.

Our relationship with Shelley stuck even when the documentary was over. In fact, it turned out to be something nobody expected. It took a while for all of us to **trust each other**—but looking back now at all we went through, **I really think we changed each other's lives.** We learned a lot about each other's different worlds and found that we're really not that different at all. Skeats and I drove her car all over the city, and Shelley did everything from type papers to cook when we were hungry. She took us to some cool stuff, too. We went to Magic Johnson's charity game at the Forum when she was able to get us some press passes because she was doing a story for ESPN on Chris Webber, who was playing in the game. That was the night I said I was his brother in order to get us into the after-party.

People still laugh at this, but *we ended up babysitting for her, too.* Her daughter, Dylann, was about five when we first met. We'd end up driving Shelley to the airport, then going and picking up Dylann from school and staying with her until Shelley or her ex-husband, Mike, got back into town. Sometimes we took Dylann over to Skeats's mom's house, and sometimes we just stayed overnight at Shelley's. We helped her, she helped us.

It was Shelley's car I used to drive alongside O.J. during his trip up the highway. And it was Shelley's car I used to get around town when I needed to. An agent she knows called her up one day, all concerned because he said I was driving a brand new gold Honda Accord, thinking I'd been bought. Little did he know, it was her car.

When I was thinking about going pro after my junior year, I talked with Shelley a lot. Skeats talked with her a lot, too, after he got a scholarship to Iowa and ended up hating the place. And Shelley talked with us about stuff, too. ESPN was trying to hire her to take a job in Chicago.

"You can't go," I told her. "Who will take care of me and Skeats?"

Really, **we all became family.** Shelley came to the ceremony for black student graduation and my football banquets. The day I was named a Walter Camp All-American, I bolted from the press conference to go speak to Dylann's fourth grade class.

Some people didn't like the article Shelley wrote on Dorsey High School. Some of it pointed out some of the **wild shit** that had gone on. We got a lot of negative attention those days. But Dorsey had some good stuff going on, too. We sent a lot of guys to college—especially in football and basketball. And look now at the guys who made it to the pros who came from Dorsey: me, Lamont Warren, Karim Abdul Jabbar, Chris Mims. So when the *SI* article came out, some people were pretty much pissed off, especially at Shelley, who had promised it would be a fair article. I guess it was fair, it was just short. It was supposed to be a good, long article, but it ran as a photo essay—using grim black-and-white pictures, which made some guys feel that they looked like **thugs—** and what she wrote was only about 100 lines.

People were seriously upset. One of them sued *Sports Illustrated* but ended up dropping the suit. Shelley got a lot of **threatening phone calls.** She took Dylann to one of our games at Compton College and some of the students confronted them in the bathroom. Some of the Dorsey mothers led a yelling attack on Shelley in the stands. It was pretty ugly.

Skeats and I didn't like the article, either. But we called her up after it came out and she explained what had happened. She was cool with us and it seemed like she was straight about the truth and all. So we decided to **defend her,** even calling up the moms and telling them to lay off. Shelley still put her red hair up in a cap and sat on the visitors' side of the stadium when she came to watch us play. It took a while, but I think things are cool now. Everybody knows what went on and why, and things are a lot different now.

I started **counting the days** left in the season after the Houston game. Damn, this year was taking a hell of a long time to get finished.

At least one thing good had happened over that weekend: USC beat Notre Dame for the first time in about a million years. It was a great game, we won in OT, and best of all, it put John Robinson right back into the driver's seat. There was no way Mike Garrett—even Mike Garrett—could fire J-Rob. They had a meeting and Robinson held out for all his assistants, too. Nobody went. Justice had been served.

Watching the game made me remember how much fun it had been to play college ball, mainly because *we were **good** and we were **winning.*** I wish I had had another year. I would have kept it, for real. Maybe I **hadn't** *grown up* to the NFL yet. It's a whole different game here, full of politics and stuff that you don't think about when you're just going to class and then to practice. I missed college ball. I missed winning and being on the front page of the sports section with a big W highlighting the day's coverage. I missed being involved in every play and getting the ball on the big downs. I missed being the go-to guy. And I couldn't figure out **why I was still lobbying** to get the ball with a 1–12 organization.

The Monday after the Houston debacle, Erhardt called a meeting with the quarterbacks. Believe it or not, the old man **finally** decided to put a play in designed just for me. We were 1–12 and the guy just figured it out? What I was supposed to do was run a pattern and get free anyway I could. Called the I-get-open-and-the-QB-finds-me pattern. Nothing fancy. Nothing tricky. Just something we should have been running all season long.

It would have been fine if Erhardt had just left it at that. But it ***must have killed him*** to stick it in. After the meeting broke up, one of the QBs (I'm not saying who because I'm not out to get him in trouble), came up to me and told me what little quip the old man had added after he diagrammed the play on the board.

"He draws it out," the QB told me. "Then says, *'Let's see if "money mouth" can pull it in.'*"

So now I was money mouth. That was funny as hell. An offensive coordinator who claims he can produce offensive results—he kept pointing to all these stats we had racked up in yardages and whatever—but an offensive coordinator who had won one game. **One game.** And he was calling me money mouth because I wanted the ball and I knew that if I started getting the ball, things were going to happen. I wasn't guaranteeing wins, but something would happen if I got the ball. He knew it. Everybody knew it. And I know it killed him to admit it. That's why he had to think up some clever little name to try to bring me down.

Glenn Foley was going to start at quarterback against New England. They had given up on Reich. Actually, I didn't think they gave up on Frank, they just wanted Foley to play so they can get somebody for him when they **TRADE HIM.**

Foley's cool, though. He likes throwing to me. He knows I'm a winner and I'm going to help this team win games. That's a fact.

So the play was in, but I wasn't going to hold my breath until the old man called it in a game.

We had a fight at practice that week, too. It was pretty funny, really. Jumbo Elliott and a bunch of the other offensive linemen started going at it and more and more guys started jumping in. At least it showed our guys **still cared about something,** even if it was kicking each other's butts.

13

PATRIOTS 34 .... Jets 10
EAGLES 21 .... Jets 20
DOLPHINS 31 .... Jets 28

I walked into the Jets' public relations office the Friday morning before our last game of the season to take a look at the day's press clippings, like I always did. Berj Najarian is one of the public relations assistants and he knew that I liked to see what crazy stuff had been written about this crazy team. But this day, instead of handing me the packet, he handed me a single sheet of paper which said that the team was calling a **major press conference** in a couple of hours.

"Uh, oh," I said. "What does this mean?"

"I guess you'll find out in a few minutes," Berj answered.

Nobody from the PR staff or front office or anywhere in the organization who knew what was going on leaked it to anyone.

Kotite was leaving.

KOTITE WAS LEAVING!!!

I couldn't believe it was actually happening. I was relieved, elated, happy. You name it. I was mainly just glad it was over. All the speculation, all the questions, all the worrying that they might keep him on another year.

Kotite called the team together, told us he was accepting responsibility for this miserable season, that the buck had to stop somewhere, and *he was **stopping it with himself.***

"I didn't get the job done," he said. "It's my fault."

And then it was over. Just like that. Kotite said he wasn't resigning and he hadn't gotten fired. So I guess he was stepping down, quitting, getting out, whatever you wanted to call it. It was done. It didn't really surprise anybody that he wouldn't be coming back, but nobody was prepared for how it all came down. All the media trucks and reporters were swarming around the building, everyone speculating about what was going on.

I guess Kotite walked into a meeting with Leon Hess and Steve Gutman and said it was time to **end all the guessing,** to get the inevitable over with. He wanted to take the pressure off of us heading into our last game and, most of all, he said, he did not want to completely alienate the Jets' fans. They had been staying home in record numbers and I really believe that hurt him. He'd been a Jets guy for a long time. Even Gutman said Kotite would always be part of the Jets' family.

Kotite's **not a bad guy.** But he's a **terrible coach** and he tries to play this tough-guy image to the hilt—smoking his cigars, talking all tough, having lots of flunkies around. I know Kotite *wants* to win. I could see it in his eyes on the sideline of each game. They were pleading with you, almost. Sometimes he looked downright desperate. I can understand why.

We were all desperate. I think it hurt him—all of us—when we'd be up in a game and then lose it in the fourth quarter. What was it about this team that caused us to just stop playing once we got a lead? It had to be something psychological. Some *funky little brain wave that said,* **"Give up now,** you know it ain't gonna happen for you today."

Kotite had just been around losing too long. He didn't know how to motivate a team to move in for the kill. We were too soft, too sensitive, and—except for Erhardt—we were too '90s. Kotite needed to step up and yell at people, get in their faces. Become a general or a dictator or something when the fourth quarter came around. Instead he just sort of *slinked along the sidelines* waiting for the inevitable. How much of it was his fault? Hell, I don't know. I don't think all of it. He didn't fumble, he didn't throw interceptions, he didn't drop passes. But somewhere, something seeped down from him to us. And it wasn't a winning attitude.

But, basically, I guess Kotite's okay as a regular guy. So in that respect **I felt a little bit sorry for the dude,** because you hate to see anyone lose a job. I think he honestly cared about the players and this organization. After his press conference, he went into his office and called his wife and kids to tell them it was over. He looked pretty sad after that. **It's a tough business.** I know that now more than ever.

Reporters crowded around my locker wanting to know what I thought. I was careful not to say too much about Kotite and tried to concentrate on the future. I talked a lot about hoping the new coach and GM would keep Richard Mann, the receivers coach. He's the only guy I really like, who I think knows how this game should be played and coached. The rest of them, well … Mann's the only one I'd really like to see stay.

I heard that I was one of only two players Kotite mentioned in the press conference. He talked about Neil O'Donnell when he was asked about all the injuries, and he talked about me when he told everyone the team had *an exciting future with some exciting players* who were bound to turn this team around. It was cool of him to say that. I hope he's right.

Kotite's departure was the culmination of a bad season gone terrible. We sucked against New England—really sucked. We were never in the game. Erhardt actually called my play a couple of times, but Foley couldn't find me. Patriots wide receiver Terry Glenn, their first-round draft choice, looked All-Pro. On stats alone, he's the rookie receiver of the year. That's because New England uses Glenn like he should be used. Bill Parcells wanted to win football games and get to the playoffs, and he did. He knows you *don't hide* a talented receiver you drafted in the first round and paid a bunch of money to. You don't make that guy a decoy, let him run up and down the field *clearing things out for some team mascot.*

Should Glenn have been picked No. 1 instead of me? Now I wish he had been. But you never know. You switch places, does it change the teams' records? Does he give the Jets seven more wins and do I make the Patriots lose more games?

Hard to tell. We were 1–13.

The Philadelphia game was a little better. At least we were competitive. Hell, **we almost won** the damn thing. How many times did I say *that* this season? We found some emotion, too. Of course, we had a little help from Eagles' quarterback Ty Detmer, who announced to the world that his team would be idiots if they lost to us. They would be. Why was that such a revelation?

Our big defensive end, Hugh Douglas, didn't agree with Detmer. In fact, **he got downright pissed and so I decided I'd get pissed, too.** We were all pissed. Hugh took it a step further, saying that if he got the chance he was going to hurt Detmer. He really didn't like Detmer's comments. I believed that he'd **stomp on the guy** given half a chance. Hugh doesn't play that.

But then everybody sort of backed off their statements. We were still pissed, though, and we played hard as hell. Maybe we ought to hire Ty Detmer as a motivational speaker next season. Hugh had the game of the season, sacking Detmer three times and recovering a fumble. I hope opposing quarterbacks continue to piss him off.

The first time Hugh got to Detmer, he sacked him hard and said, "It's going to be a long day."

We heard him on the sidelines and laughed our asses off. There was **a lot of trash-talking going on** during the game. When Hugh recovered the fumble, he pointed to the Eagles' sidelines and yelled: "It isn't going to be easy."

And it wasn't. We were ahead the entire game and ended up losing 21–20. Yes, we found another way to lose a lead and lose a game. We were entertaining, if nothing else.

I knew Kotite wanted this one bad. The night before the game he called us all together and gave us one of those Lombardi-like speeches. **Only problem was, he WASN'T Lombardi.** He talked to us about pride and emotion and told us how the Philadelphia management had treated him badly, openly courting Jimmy Johnson while he was still on the Philly payroll. He wanted payback. It just didn't happen.

We had five turnovers. **You don't beat a team of NUNS with five turnovers.** The play-calling, again, was messed up. I had four catches for 77 yards, giving me 60 receptions on the season. The touchdown pass I caught was another flea-flicker, which caught the Eagles sleeping. All of a sudden I was 37 yards up the field and the ball floated right into my hands. That was sweet.

But other stuff was crazy. We were up 20–14 with six minutes left in the game. Erhardt calls a hitch-and-go to Richie Anderson. Anderson hitched and went, but Foley threw to the hitch spot and the Eagles' Mike Zordich picked it off. It was the wrong play to call at that time in the game. Foley was young and inexperienced, and it was a risky play when we could have just hammered it out on the ground and used up the clock.

Oh, well.

I went up to Hugh and shook his hand. *I loved the way he played.*

"If it doesn't happen this next game, we're going to make it happen in 1997," I told him.

I meant it, too. If we ended up 1–15, it was going to piss us off and get us even hungrier next season. I will not let this happen again, believe me.

I was surprised to see a lot of our fans come back for the Miami game. People were even tailgating. I guess they were happy with Kotite's decision and decided to cut him a little slack, since he didn't drag the issue out forever. I have to admit **he did show a lot of class** by taking the responsibility and doing the right thing. It had to be tough.

The signs in the stands were hilarious.

THE END OF AN ERROR, read one, and HORRIBLE EVERY SINGLE SEASON. Take the first letter of those four words and you come up with H-E-S-S, the name of our fearless owner. He showed up at the game, but didn't say a whole lot. Big surprise there. I heard the dude had a wonderful speech at Thanksgiving last year where he implored the team to finish the season without "acting like a bunch of **horses' asses."**

So I was all geared up for the speech this Thanksgiving, but it wasn't close to his performance in 1995.

The $25 million man made an appearance at the game, too, after not bothering to come to the Philadelphia game.

"It's hard on his leg for him to stand," Kotite explained.

I still want to see the medical report on that calf muscle.

Foley was starting again, something I still couldn't figure out. Had we just given up on any chance of winning another game? Everyone knew Reich was ten times the quarterback Foley was. But they said they wanted Foley to get the work. Hell, might as well just put in the entire third team so they can get the work.

I needed seven catches to break the Jets' record for rookie receivers. But I knew immediately I wasn't even going to get seven balls thrown my way. Guess who held the record? Right. **Richie's mascot.** Chrebet had 66 receptions in 1995 and there was no way they were going to let me take that from him. I might as well have just sat out. I still haven't figured out the **love connection** between Kotite and Chrebet. I think Wayne probably reminds Richie of himself. Chrebet's a good player, I'll give him that. But he's not even a No. 3 receiver, and the Jets have made him All-World.

Our last game of the season started with a bang. A big bang. Big Hugh Douglas scooped up a fumble and ran it 62 yards for a touchdown. He was happy as hell and actually looked kind of fast out there. Well, as fast as somebody 6'2" and 265 pounds can look. We were up 7–0 and then we went up 14–0 when Adrian Murrell ran the ball in one yard for another TD. Actually, Adrian fumbled out of bounds before he broke the plane, but the referee gave it to him anyway. Adrian hugged him after that. *That was funny as hell, seeing a player hug the ref.* I think it stunned him.

But then, just like that, the Dolphins caught us. And once again, they caught us mainly because of the play of my old roommate, Karim Abdul Jabbar, who ran his ass off. He carried the ball *30 times for 152 yards and went over the 1,000-yard mark* for the year. He had a remarkable season and I know that team's going somewhere next year. I saw Jimmy Johnson before the game and, once again, begged him to find a way to get me to Miami. He just laughed. I'm not sure he thought I was serious.

"You'll be okay," he kept saying.

I wasn't so sure.

Miami went up 31–21 in the fourth quarter and it

started looking like another big L for us. That was until *Kotite decided he'd seen* **enough** *of Foley* and sent Reich in at quarterback. Foley was pissed as hell.

"How can you do that?" Foley screamed at Kotite on the sideline.

"I just did it," Kotite yelled back.

I told Foley later to pay no attention to it.

"You should have thrown me the ball," I said. "I'd have made sure you stayed in the game."

With Reich back, so was our energy. He's a far better quarterback than Foley and the $25 million man put together. I felt like we'd get something done now and we did, moving the ball upfield and getting ourselves into scoring position. Reich overthrew me once in the end zone, then nailed Chrebet with a nine-yard pass to pull us within three points with 4:45 left in the game.

Chrebet held onto the ball and then ran over and **gave it to Kotite.** Sweet.

We got the ball back after Bobby Hamilton sacked Dan Marino. We had it first-and-10 on our own 37 and we had some confidence and momentum going. Reich dropped back and launched a 14-yard pass to Chrebet, who turned upfield and … fumbled. Game over. Season over.

"I tried to play this game differently and I think I hurt myself," Chrebet said to the media later. "It was like my Super Bowl out there and I wanted more than anything to win this one for Richie. I think I tried to play outside myself a little bit and I think I hurt the team. I take a lot of the blame."

Kotite came out of the locker room and addressed the media, **defending the Mascot** before anyone even asked.

"I love Wayne Chrebet," he said. "He's going to become one of the best players in this league."

Chrebet wouldn't even make anybody else's team. ***It was time to stop this love affair with the little dude from Hofstra.***

"Big-game players make big plays in big games," I told Austin Murphy from *Sports Illustrated*. "This was supposedly a big game. That's all I can say."

Marvin Washington was talking mess, too.

"Next time I come here, I want to be in the dressing room down the hall," he said, meaning the visitors' side of things.

I talked to Karim after the game. He laughed pretty hard when he learned what the title of this book would be.

"Very appropriate," he said.

"Very true," I said back.

And so the season is over. I'm glad it's finished. Everything we've been through, oh, my God, what an embarrassment. I told the reporters standing around my locker that I was excited to find out who the new coaches were going to be and to get to know them. No repeats of this stuff next year. I'm lobbying right here and right now. Get me the ball. **Get it to me EARLY and get it to me OFTEN.** I'll take you places.

I walked out of the locker room and towards the exit. I stopped, reached down and dug through my bag and found my bright green vinyl Jets playbook. I grabbed it and walked right over to the nearest trash can and stuffed it hard.

"This shit is over," I said.

It is.

Then I hopped in the limo that had brought all my friends and family to the game. Usually we go somewhere in the city to get some grub. This time, though, *all I wanted to do was get home, get packed, and get the hell out of New York.* I saw some cool stuff this season. I went to the play "Miss Saigon," and I went to a lot of poppin' clubs and parties—the best one was thrown by Motown in the beginning of the season. I made some lifelong friends. Jeff Graham is talking about moving to L.A. in the off-season, coming out West to hang with me and my crew. That would be great.

I'm **tired** and **frustrated** and **embarrassed** that things didn't get done this year. But I'm already ready for next season. I'm going to work out harder than ever. I'm going to catch passes from anybody who'll throw to me. I'm going to play with my daughter and move my entire family into the house I'm building in the Valley. We're going to barbeque every night and swim every day. Hell, I might even learn how to play golf.

Draft day seems like a lifetime ago. On draft day I was happy as hell to have been chosen No. 1 and to be coming to the New York Jets. People warned me about this team. All I can say is that they were right. I've got four or five more years here, though. And I'm not letting up on anyone—teammates, coaches, fans—until we get it right. It's time for the losing to stop.

I can't wait until next year.

Index

Printed in the United States
145687LV00002B/5/A

9 780446 521451